The Alignment of the Universe:

Messages From Other Worlds

Channelled by Victoria Cochrane

To Richy.
My husband,
my twin flame
and my life-long love.

Preface

In 2012, I conducted a 12 week spiritual development course. There were eight participants who have all gone on to become my spiritual family. At that time I was writing my first book. One evening, as I was going over some of my channellings, the light in the kitchen flickered. Knowing that a light flickering is usually a sign that someone in spirit wants my attention, I quickly took myself into a Theta state to see who it was. To my surprise there were twelve masters standing in the kitchen. I could see them in colour, all wearing robes of various shades and some wearing turbans or head attire. I greeted them and asked to what I deserved the honour of their visit? They informed me that they were Masters from 'The Circle of Illumination', or Light, and were coming in at this time to assist me with my group, most of whom were destined to be important Earth healers.

I was extremely honoured and excited, and proceeded to ask for all of their names, so I could inform my group when it was appropriate to do so. The members of the Circle of Illumination are as follows: Kuan Yin, Christopher Columbus, Buddha, Mary Magdalene, Archeia Faith, Archangel Sandalphon, Master Demetrius, Mother Teresa, Master Abel, Master Josiah and Master Lauriellus. Now, seven months after they joined me, and after I had witnessed the alignment of Mother Earth with other solar systems in the universe on the 21st December, 2012, it was Master Demetrius who was the first delegate to take on my continuing education. He told me that he came to teach me the higher truths of the universe, of the ways of our sister planets and how to connect to them so they can download important information that can help us in our quest to ascend. As the channelling of this book continued slowly over the next two years, more Masters joined him to bring in the information that constitutes this book. I thank them all for the love and patience: Master Demetrius, Archangel Michael, Master Kathumi, Jesus, Lord Mekchizadek, Unos of the Siriun High Council, Svelta Devo of the Arcturun High Council, Frier Manus, also a member of the Arcturun High Council and delegate for the Intergalactic Federation and Master Kokunus, a representative of the Pleiades cluster.

During the writing of this book I visited the four planets described in this book in meditations. I was also shown the Siriun Blue Flame before the chapter was given to me, and I have used the Capsule of Wisdom in conjunction with my higher self to answer questions my logical mind could not. In another meditation, before I channelled the chapter, I found myself in the centre of the sun watching funny little beings bounce around in the darkness. I was, to my amazement, meeting the Sun People!

Many of the terms and discussions in this book have been introduced in my first two books, published in 2013 (Balboa Press). The Masters have not explained them again, so there may be a need to refer to them as you read. They are both available online as hard copies and e-books and are titled, "Raising the Energies of Mother Earth Towards and After Ascension 2012: The Highest Truth," and "Beyond Ascension 2012: Universal Truths."

I am not sure if the Earth is ready for the messages in this book and for the truths that it unveils, however, I fear more for the consequences of not publishing it. I fully trust in the love, support and protection of the Supreme Creator and the Masters of Light in the creation and publication of these messages. I also thank my family, friends and regular clients for their support and encouragement as the time it took to write the book lengthened. My love, heartfelt gratitude and blessings go to them and to all of you as we all travel the road of ascension together. May we all one day know only oneness, peace, and total harmony on Earth. I hope that you can all read these messages with an open mind and heart, and I also hope that you can begin to experience the joy, love and wonder of the universe and the ethereal kingdom as I have.

The Creator of All That Is is the Supreme Source, Mother/Father God and is neither male nor female. For the sake of continuity all references are male.

Many blessings,
Victoria Cochrane, 2015.

Foreword

I first met Victoria Cochrane on the telephone; it was early 2013. I was searching for a "healer" and stumbled across Theta® Healing on the internet. I scrolled through plenty of different Theta® Healers from everywhere, but Victoria felt like the one I needed to contact. In fact, I felt as though I already knew her.

I had no idea how it would work with Victoria living in Tasmania and our family temporarily located in Perth, Western Australia at the time, but I trusted it would. Our then, 7 year old daughter, Alyssa had a terminal brain tumour and we were struggling. Victoria played an instrumental part in our lives with her gifted skill as a Theta® Healer. She helped to assist Alyssa at a traumatic time and then went on to help us to grieve and stay strong for each other after her passing. She continues to assist me with my spiritual development today.

It was not until 2014 that I would actually meet Victoria in person in Darwin and I felt like we were old friends just catching up — it felt right. I knew our friendship would be forever.

I've gained knowledge and understanding from the channellings in her books and I have gained an incredible mentor and best friend. The first two books are fantastic and this one will be equally insightful and compelling, if not more.

Victoria is an amazing Theta® Healer and author, and an incredibly kind and compassionate person. She's my "Sister."

Angela Spackman

Table of Contents

Preface..i

Foreward iii

Part 1: Unveiling Secrets of the Universe 1

Chapter 1: The Creation of the Universe 3

Chapter 2: Beginnings.. 7

Chapter 3: The Second Coming 11

Chapter 4: The Sun 15

Chapter 5: Reclaiming Your God-Self... 21

Chapter 6: The Universal Mind: 27

Chapter 7: Traversing Time and Space 31

Chapter 8: The War on the Astral Plane 35

Chapter 9: The Crystalline Grid.. 39

Part 2: The Inter-Planetary Galactic Federation............................ 43

Chapter 10: The Inter-Planetary Galactic Federation 45

Chapter 11: Orion.. 49

Chapter 12: Sirius 55

Chapter 13: The Siriun Blue Flame 59

Chapter 14: Arcturus.. 61

Chapter 15: Tourous.. 65

Chapter 16: The Pleiades 69

Part 3: The Keys to Ascension 73

Chapter 17: Rising Above the Ego 75

Chapter 18: Oneness 83

Chapter 19: Learning to Just Be 91

Chapter 20: New Beginnings 95

About the Author 99

PART 1
Unveiling Secrets of the Universe

CHAPTER 1
The Creation of the Universe

All matter is grounded in creation, for how can it exist if it at first was not created? The creation of the universe has evolved over eons of time, but the fact that there was matter to begin with is the question we wish to ponder here. How is it that the fine particles that make up all things existed in the first place? Was there a 'Big Bang' that created the planets, stars and moons that exist today? Did God just wave his staff and create the world in a week as the Christians believe?

Matter is energy. Anything that exists in the world and the universe has been created through energy and thus vibrates energetically at its own natural rate. The creation of the universe can, indeed, be credited to the Supreme Source but not in the way Christians describe. The universe was created by energy colliding with itself and forming solid matter. In a space with no restrictions on speed or distance, the existence of energy and the manner in which it was travelling was destined to create matter of substance that began microscopically-small but built upon itself exponentially until the matter began to clump, stick together and form solid formations.

The Supreme Creator is an energetic force that creates with loving intention. The Supreme Mother/Father God is an energy of light and essence that is of no substance but which has a consciousness of love and light that literally breathes life into anything it gives mind to. The particles of creation are called 'Adamantine Particles' and are the substance behind all matter that has ever been created. They are the energy behind the creation; the life-force energy that is responsible for all matter coming into being. The intention behind each creation determines the frequency at which it vibrates, and that is true with anything that is created by any human today.

Throughout the continued evolvement of galaxies, solar systems, planets and stars within the universe, the vibration behind each creation has been of unconditional love and the utmost respect for every living creature and non-living element taking form. In the creation of living and non-living matter a symbiosis of existence was developed and still evolves today, ensuring that no one element stands alone and that all life-forms will receive the nourishment they need to grow and survive. A natural hierarchy of existence is the way of many planets, beginning with a simple food chain up to a complex eco-system, but it is not the way of all planets in the many galaxies making up the universal structure. The one underlying force of all existence are the adamantine particles of creation, and the only vibration that can be applied to them is love — that is all there ever has been in the universe and all there ever will be. Therefore, the name, 'The Creator of All That Is' signifies that God, or The Supreme Source, holds this energy and will only ever create in the energy of unconditional love and oneness with all.

The Supreme Creator's energy is one of fact and truth — there is no fluffiness to the messages that he gives to the world. In the energy of the Creator there is no room for illusion, lies or betrayal, and when one creates in his energy the vibration will be of the utmost integrity. All matter, whether it is living or non-living is one with the Creator and has been created with the adamantine particles of creation; therefore, everything that exists in the universe is a thing of love and unblemished beauty. The perfection of creation is only lost through experiences that are of a lower vibration than which the object or being was first created. So, when humans experience conditional love, harsh environments and emotions such as hatred and betrayal, they may either become a product of their environment or damaged because of it. However, their unspoilt beauty at the time of conception (or creation), is still a spark within them — it is written in every human's DNA. That is why Creator will always tell you that you are perfect with nothing to change, even though you may actually feel broken inside. Conditioning from societal expectations and from harsh judgements from self and others can cause a human being to consider that they do not belong in the world and to take their own life. The energy of judgement is not in the vibration of oneness and should never be attributed to the judgement, wrath or will of God. The only energy that can ever be attributed to God is unconditional love, which constitutes acceptance, peace and total oneness with Him.

All humans are one with the light, are born of the light and go back to the light at the end of their incarnation on Earth. The physical body is merely a vessel for the spirit of the soul to evolve and grow through lessons it has chosen to learn. Nothing is real but love, so all drama that is played out on the Earthly Plane is an illusion that has the potential to keep a spirit firmly grounded in the physical body, denying the spiritual connection that is rightfully theirs.

To feel connected to Source is a right, not a privilege. There is no need for religious restrictions, for one cannot put a restriction on love. There are no rules or boundaries around God's love, for the Creator just is, so therefore love also just is. You have come into being through a moment in time where the adamantine particles collided. You have been created, and you continuously create through every moment in time with every decision, word and deed that you do and make. You are a co-creator and one with creation. You are a being of love who instinctively knows that the world is an illusion and to be enjoyed for a time before you return to the light to continue your wondrous soul journey to enlightenment and mastery.

CHAPTER 2
Beginnings

Jesus came to Earth at a time when this planet was aligned with others in the universe. His message was universal and was heard far and wide, not just on Earth — it was heard in other galaxies and solar systems. The impact of his message, that God is love and light, and of his selfless sacrifice, was felt by beings on other planets and is still lovingly remembered.

This time has passed, however, and we are now in a time when many people on Earth are stuck firmly in the past. They still focus on the sacrifice Jesus made, yet they cannot see into the future beyond what has been written in the Bible. They wait for Jesus to walk the Earth, yet they do not recognize the many aspects of Jesus walking the Earth at this time. They also fail to recognise how the love of Jesus can be felt in their heartspace simply by uttering his name.

The alignment of the universe on the 21/12/12 has allowed other worlds to begin to share their knowledge with humans on Earth that they have learnt over the ages from the universal Christ Consciousness. They have watched the decline of the human consciousness with interest and dismay, but without judgement. They recognise that humans have an ego and the right to exercise their free will, but the coming of Jesus has been lost in religious doctrine and endless boundaries that restrict, rather than enhance, peoples' abilities to know and feel God's love.

The wisdom gained by knowing Christ through his consciousness, rather than merely his physical presence, has been immense in other worlds. The alien way of life is foreign to that on Earth because it is entirely peaceful; it is one of unity, oneness and total absence of ego. This enables beings on almost every other planet in the universe to exist in love and without the presence of hatred, war, or feelings of competition. They know themselves and their life's purpose from birth. They live to serve their communities and each other. They communicate through telepathy and through their heartspace. They are one with Source and they live their truth with honesty, integrity and unconditional love.

Beings from other worlds do not comprehend the thoughts and emotions of man on Earth. They do not exist in a state of ego, so they cannot understand lower emotions of hatred, lust, greed, corruption and envy. In other worlds the living beings exist for their community — they are a colony, if you wish, where all deeds serve the greater good of all. In this way, their thoughts and deeds are united as one, and they are all working towards the same end. All members of the community are 'on the same page' as you say. There is a higher plan and they all know it, work towards it, and believe in it.

Humans on Earth have met many aliens. There have been chance meetings and there have been planned ones. The existence of life on other planets has long been the wonderings of man, but some humans have discovered their existence and worked to make this knowledge to their own advantage. Make no bones about it, not all alien visits have been friendly, nor have they been for the greater good of mankind on Earth, but this is not entirely the fault of the aliens in question. Many humans in higher ranks saw the chance to profit and to gain power over other worlds, and they would stop at nothing to do so. In allowing aliens to conduct research on Earth, they were gaining valuable insights into life on the aliens' planets, their technology and their gifts. There was not an equal exchange of energy in the contract, and many aliens were exterminated after they had completed their side of the bargain.

The events of the past have made your universal neighbours wary, and they have learnt much about the human mind, which they consider to be banal and altruistic. They hold no fear or grudge, for their time on Earth has been a great lesson for them. However, they know that if Earth continues on its present path of self-destruction, the impact on their own planets and beyond will be immeasurable, and this is a risk they cannot allow. Instead of taking over and invading, which was never their way, they are now using the alignment within the universe to traverse the distance and to send you their wisdom in an attempt to raise vibrations amongst the masses and to bring Earth fully into its ascended state.

On the 12/12/2012 the Earth ascended from the Third Dimension into the Fifth, raising its vibrations out of the mire of negativity, despair, hatred and war that it has been languishing in for so long. There was an awakening around that time of many people around the world who began to realise that the world's religions are vastly lacking in their explanations of life beyond the physical world and that their teachings of separatism and the vengeance of God are largely to blame for the clash of, rather than acceptance and tolerance of, different beliefs on Earth. For man to reach the ascended state in which Mother Earth now sits, every individual must work to rise above the self-serving inclinations of the ego and begin to see the world from a higher perspective. All people, animals, living and non-living things on Earth are connected: to Mother Earth, to each other and to the Creator. Indeed, they are connected to everything in the universe that makes up the all. Separatism is but an illusion, and when oneness is accepted as a reality ascension to the Fifth Dimension will be achieved.

The benefits of Earth reaching and maintaining a Fifth Dimensional state will not be restricted to humans on Earth. This event will bring Earth into alignment with its brother and sister planets who live in harmony and whose planets are not out of reach to humans who are in their ethereal state. Many of you have lived in these worlds and many of you will return back to them once your incarnation on Earth is complete.

We cannot stress enough how important the messages coming through from these other worlds are at this time. Take notice of thoughts that are not your own, repeated symbols and dreams. Be aware of those around you and the messages they deliver to you in their speech. Listen and look for signs that will help you to assimilate this higher knowledge into your being. The more people who do this, the higher the vibrations on Earth will be, and all who exist in the universe will benefit.

And so it is.

CHAPTER 3
The Second Coming

Emotions are running high in the world at this present time, as many changes are taking place on cellular levels within humans whose consciousness has become awakened. Some of you have been aware of the impending changes and have been ready for them, however, many have been caught unawares and are finding it difficult to cope. The changes are, indeed, associated with the ascension of Mother Earth on the 12/12/12, yet there are other changes that are occurring as part of evolution and as adaption to life on the planet.

Ascension has been foretold since before Jesus came to Earth. The second coming is upon the world, yet it is not as has been prophesised by Christians. The saviour of the world this time is not the return of the saviour, Jesus, in person but the raising of human vibrations to a Fifth Dimensional state: one of peace, tolerance, unconditional love and total acceptance of each other. Humans must all do their part to make the changes in their thought patterns and vibrations to allow the world to continue on her path to ascension.

The other changes that are occurring are evolutionary; they are adaptations to environment but also to temperament. People raising their vibrations to the ascended state are aligning to the crystalline grid and bringing in their crystalline Lightbodies. One cannot move back into their Lightbody* without some major physical and structural changes taking place. Those whose bodies are adjusting to the major changes in vibrational patterns in the universe, not just on Earth, are finding that the changes in their physical bodies and mental abilities are becoming apparent — they are becoming more sensitive to the world around them, unable to tolerate harsh chemicals; they eat more raw and organic food and avoid processed food; they may eat less or no meat. These humans are more aware of ecological issues and are becoming more protective and proactive in their attitudes to the preservation of nature. Their bodies are becoming stronger and finer, their lifestyles healthier. Their minds are much more alert at the time of birth and they reach milestones earlier. Their spiritual essence is apparent from the day of birth and, contrary to earlier generations, will stay a strong influence throughout the lives of the newest generations. There is a tendency now to steer away from prejudicial thinking and intolerance, and the use of war and violence as a way of solving differences is increasingly being rejected and abhorred. These vibrational changes may seem innocent and obscure, but they are not just a reaction to recent occurrences on Earth. They actually stem back much further and are changing the cellular structure of the human body and the human psyche in ways that will be much more apparent as the days move closer to the full ascension of Earth.

If you feel different to the way you used to be, go within and instruct your body to accept and assimilate the light that is now entering your energy fields. Become aware of your chakras and aura and actively seek to keep their energies clear and unblocked. Learn how to protect your energy fields against attack and from absorbing or trading with other peoples' energies. The more you do now to seek connection with your own energies and with the energies of ascension, the higher your vibrations will rise and, along with them, the vibrations of those around you. All is connected. When you assimilate the positive changes occurring and begin to actively seek your spiritual connection, the world will respond in kind.

The changes occurring are not just restricted to the human body. The weather patterns around the world have, in many cases, become unpredictable and unseasonable. There are storms when there should be calm, ice and snow when there should be sunshine, and rain in unusual times of the year. There have been many cyclones and tempests that have been vicious in their nature and the havoc they have wreaked has been out of the ordinary and quite unexpected. Some areas have experienced continuous or regular flooding, and other areas are unseasonably dry.

There are many causes for disruptions to the weather and all of them are linked in some way. The major cause of change in weather and climate is the presence of man on Earth. Humans have lived and plundered the Earth and put many pollutants and toxins into the environment and atmosphere. Climate change is not a figment of anyone's imagination but a cold, hard fact. One cannot expect that the environment, that is so sensitive and finely interwoven in its cycles and patterns, cannot be affected by constant exposure to chemicals, toxins, poisons and dense populations! The presence of humans is the reason there is so much imbalance upon the Earth, although humans have always been welcomed and assisted to exist there.

Indigenous populations who claim first habitation of the Earth were less invasive on her resources and did not pollute as modern man has done, that is true. However, their claim that the land is rightfully theirs is a fallacy. The land belongs to no-one, as it is a part of the all and is therefore a part of creation, as is man and all that can be seen and touched upon the planet. All that exists and has been created just is, and any claim to ownership comes through ego and self-service rather than a wish to contribute to the greater good. All that Mother Earth provides is given freely with no restriction or discrimination on the proviso that an exchange of energy is received and that all is treated with the utmost respect and reverence. If no such exchange occurs an imbalance is created. Lack of respect for the Earth indicates that man lacks respect for himself and his fellow humans. There is no dignity in living upon an Earth that is treated disrespectfully, and one cannot expect Mother Earth to return any form of energy as exchange higher than that which she is given.

Foul and savage weather is one of the returns of energy from Mother Earth when she has not been treated with respect and dignity. A drying up or withholding of resources, such as drought or famine, is another manifestation of such treatment. Floods and tempest are an attempt by Mother Earth to expunge corruption and desecration from her surface and her body. Repeated attempts at purging may indicate there has been extreme savagery, bloodshed, pillaging and/or disrespect in that area in the past.

Human emotions are also reflected in the weather, and where there is much negativity, such as in war zones, the weather will seem extremely harsh at times. It may be blazing hot, freezing cold or very blustery and windy — there will be extremes in temperature and in weather patterns more often than not. Instability and fragility in human emotions and the psyche will affect the weather and also the human collective consciousness because the power of thought cannot be underestimated. Harsh words and deeds will manifest from toxic thought processes and, because all upon the Earth is one, every thought, word and deed is united and a powerful force towards mass negativity or positivity. Never fall under the illusion that what you think, do or say cannot affect other people or other parts of the world. All humans are united spiritually as a part of the all and can thus consider themselves family to every individual on the planet.

Lightworkers and Wayshowers can do much good for the Earth at this time by sending light and love to the areas that are worst affected by human greed, ego and abuse. The power of prayer and meditation in asking for healing upon the Earth is a force for good that cannot be underestimated, and when groups of like-minded individuals join with intent to send loving healing to the planet the impact will be greater than one could ever imagine. More than ever before the Masters urge you to join forces with your friends and colleagues to pray, meditate and send love and healing to the Earth daily. You may feel drawn to a particular place or element, or you may just hold the energy for the whole planet. Whatever or wherever it is you are drawn to send your love to will benefit from the energy. Use your thought processes for good and send loving thoughts out, even to those you would rather avoid.

The power of love is a force to be reckoned with as it is aligned to the light of the Creator; therefore the saviour of the world is love! The masters and angelic kingdom will be ready to assist you to magnify the energy that you send — all you need to do is ask. Seek help from another Lightworker if you must, but know that we, the Masters, are with you at this time as you move through time and space into another dimension; one of peace, trust, goodwill and unconditional love. We urge you to answer the call of ascension. It is the only way to save your planet from destruction.

It is, indeed, the second coming.

And so it is.

* For more information on the Lightbody see
"Raising the Energies of Mother Earth Towards and After Ascension 2012: The Highest Truth." (Cochrane, 2013, Balboa Press).

CHAPTER 4
The Sun

The sun is a star that is many millions of kilometres away from the Earth. It warms your planet and gives life to plants and animals. It is as necessary as air, because without the sun there would be no life or growth. The power of the sun is at times destructive to living things on Earth. Although Earth is the only planet in its solar system that is conducive to sustaining multitudes of life forms, there are places where the sun's rays are either too close or too far away to sustain life without adaptation or extreme challenge. The Earth is, in this way, both an easy and an extremely difficult place to live. Animals and humans adapt in different ways according to the living conditions, and ways of life vary according to the location, climate and temperatures. The power of the sun to either sustain or end life cannot be underestimated or miscalculated, nor should its power for healing be forgotten or dismissed. The sun, therefore, is the ruler of life on Earth and the activities that can be engaged in according to the weather, the seasons and the location. It is integral to life and death, and the central focus of the solar system.

The intense heat of the sun prohibits humans going anywhere near it in physical form, but its energy and its messages are accessible to you at any time. It is possible to go inside the sun, to sit on its surface amidst the fire and the intense heat and to see the beings that actually reside there. The sun is, in fact, a keeper of life and a source of intense healing and power. There are many secrets that the sun holds that she will give to you willingly, should you visit and ask. The sun is, of course, not the only star that provides warmth and life to its solar system in the way Earth's does. It is not even the oldest star, yet the life that it keeps and the energy that it gives is sacred and pure, and would be of immense benefit to all who take the opportunity to avail themselves of her gifts.

The sun comes into alignment with the Earth four times a day at each point of direction: north, south, east and west. These are the best times that humans can use the sun's rays for healing and regeneration of cells. There is no need to be directly in contact with the sun's rays or heat as it is possible to connect to the sun's energy in meditation and direct it through your body. Master Kathumi explains these teachings further and gifts to you a meditation to try:

"Stars have properties just as the Earth or the moon does. Stars, such as your sun, are constantly burning energy, whereas planets and moons store it as well as use it. The energy of the sun is a life force that cannot be underestimated, but its uses are not just for heat and generation of life. The life force of the sun represents Creation itself, and, when focused upon in the mind's eye, will go as far as regenerating cells and renewing tissue. Your belief system must be such that you believe it to be so, and your energy must be clear enough to receive this renewable energy. It is best done at the beginning of the day, when the air is fresh and the sun's rays are weakest as your body will receive the energy more efficiently then. However, if you cannot do it then, take yourself back to the morning time on the timeline, or ask that the energy you are receiving is from that part of the day. It will be done.

Be seated where you are most comfortable. It is not necessary to be in the sun's rays, for your attention and intention will be enough. Close your eyes and centre yourself in your heartspace. Connect to the ground and to the Creator. Then, in your mind's eye, see the sun as a glorious ball of heat and life-force energy. Align yourself to this energy, and hold the intention that this energy enter your body wherever it is needed to regenerate cells, renew tiwssue and accelerate healing. Hold this intention and witness or feel the sun's life-force enter your being. When it is done, re-centre yourself, ground and reconnect with the Creator. Give thanks and blessings for the gifts you have received."

The sun is a place of residence for beings who live under the rule of the Sun God. They worship the sun and its ruler and regenerate the sun's energy as it is expended. These beings are the Sun People and they live in the darkness of the sun's core. They float and bounce up and down continuously, never remaining still. Their bodies are composed of carbon and gases, and they do not need to eat or drink as the sun's energy replenishes them. The Sun God is larger and in command of his subjects. He holds the energy for them all. His role is both of ruler and protector. There are no decisions to be made, just energy to send and restore. The Sun People are peaceful and fully isolated. They speak to no-one unless a master takes his energy into their space, which they allow in the name of love. All suns that sustain life in their solar system are home to this life-form.

As Master Kathumi explains, stars such as your sun are continuously burning energy. Therefore, they must eventually burn out. When they do, the Sun People do not die straight away. They cluster together, gathering gases and particles left over from the star. It forms a crust over them where they finally stop existing. They then form a part of the universe that cannot be erased. It is a natural part of cyclic return as on your Earth; death and life are intertwined and are a progression of existence that is never ending. New stars are formed when universal gases and particles conglomerate together over millions of years. In turn, it takes hundreds of millions of years for stars to burn out. The length of time that it takes to build planetary bodies is incomprehensible to the human mind, however, as the universe does not operate on the basis of time, the state of the universe and the formation of it just is.

Life forms that have no solid physical body may seem like a fantasy, but their existence and abilities to communicate intelligently with each other is a fact, such as The Shadow People as described in the previous chapter. They form an important part of the fabric of life within the universe, much the same as plankton form the basis for life within the oceans of the Earth. All life, after all, is made up of energy, and energy is expended and replenished in a continuous cycle. In human terms, to be living relies upon the consumption and expenditure of energy through a system that constantly renews and replenishes itself. The life form may or may not have a heartbeat, and it may or may not move. Nevertheless, the exchange of gases, thought-forms and other matter, whether physical or not, into the environment means that it is, of essence, alive. So it is with non-physical beings that exist in various places and forms in the universe.

The sun is a powerful force whose energies are magnetic, healing and, at times, destructive. The sun's solar flares and magnetic forces have a strong bearing on the weather, the tides and even the human consciousness on Earth, but this strong energy ebbs and flows according to the rate of energy burned by the sun and also by the molten activity deep below the Earth's crust. Nothing is separate, all is connected and all life is affected by the changes occurring within the human consciousness that, in turn, affects the vibrations being emitted both from the sun and from Mother Earth herself.

There are many frequencies emitting from the Earth's surface. Vibrational patterns filtering around the Earth can be confused and confusing. Mother Earth herself vibrates at different frequencies in different parts of the world according to the amount of love-energy that humans allow to flow in from the Creator. There are many areas that have been tainted by darkness, ego, greed, hatred and bloodshed that are now repelling Creator's light and that are emitting very low frequencies that easily attract low entities and negative energies. The people living in these areas are most likely to be caught up in dense dramas and the lowest of human emotions that will continue to perpetuate the cycles of violence, hatred and war. In other areas of the planet where there are pockets of religious or spiritual people emitting higher vibrations of tolerance, love and good will, the energies are much higher and lighter, allowing the Adamantine Particles of creation to permeate the Earth and all living things. In this way there is no balance on Earth in terms of vibrational frequencies, and there are, as a consequence, many people who may never find their way out of the lower levels of the Third Dimension unless they receive significant help from those who are already living and working in and of the light.

There are also frequencies and magnetic vibrations being emitted from the sun, and sometimes they clash with those coming from Earth. The power and the force of magnetism on human health and well-being cannot be over-stated. In fact, there have been many cases on Earth where humans have developed mental and physical illnesses because of the imbalances in their organs caused by magnetic deficiencies. On other planets, the peaceful state that living in oneness creates has a stabilising effect on the magnetic attraction and polarisation of bodily functions and organs in alignment with the planet and the sun's. The stability of the planet's mental and physical health also has a reciprocal effect on the stability of magnetic forces being emitted from within the planet and from the central energy source. All is aligned and all is in balance. In terms of ascension, then, magnetic forces have a very large part to play on whether the living population can maintain the mental clarity and physical well-being that is required to sustain a Fifth Dimensional state. In many cases, the effects of the full moon on people's health, sleep and moods can actually be attributed to magnetic forces from the sun.

There is much one can do to align oneself to the magnetic and polar forces that criss-cross the Earth and that also emit from the sun. It is vital that all humans become aware of how they are effected by magnetism and whether it is necessary to adjust the energies around and within them to attract or repel magnetic forces as needed. To offset the impact of supercharged magnetic energies being emitted from the sun it may, at certain times, be necessary to wear magnetic devices or to use electronic equipment that can negate the effects felt upon the individual's body and psyche. It may also be necessary to limit the number of devices that use magnetic energy if anyone finds they are especially sensitive to it. If your body is not working efficiently and is severely disrupted, a natural health practitioner may be able to help you to re-polarise your energies and to re-align to magnetic fields, balancing the negative and positive ions in your body. The most powerful way, however, is to simply align your energies to the sun and to accept its healing presence. Through the Creator of All That Is, see the sun in your mind's eye and ask that your magnetic fields be polarised and aligned to the sun's magnetic fields for your highest and best. See, feel, or sense the alignment happening. You will feel the difference straight away.

Working with the sun is an invigorating and powerful way of renewing and regenerating cells. It is, however, best done at the beginning of the day and as a regular practice in your meditations. Ask the Creator and Masters of Light to assist you. You will be amazed at the benefits

CHAPTER 5
Reclaiming Your God-Self

The alignment of worlds has occurred and then passed, but the channel for the relaying of information to Earth has remained. Awareness of the availability of universal knowledge and information from other worlds who were in alignment has been given to Lightworkers on Earth who have chosen to be the Wayshowers for others. For their service the Masters of Light are grateful, because the quest towards enlightenment and ascension has been a long and often difficult process, which without the grounding of ethereal, angelic and divine energy through the physical, human form would make the process untenable. Those who have already awakened to their God-self are tireless in their efforts to assist others in their awakening and to step into their Divine selves. All is given and all is available, because it is every human's right to return to their Lightbody and to experience the joy and bliss that oneness with the all brings.

There are seven planets aligned to the Inter-Planetary Galactic Federation with members who are now willing to assist Mother Earth and her people in the quest to attain a permanent Fifth Dimensional State. Their messages of love and hope in this document are also intermingled with their own stories and advice. We cannot stress enough to those who are awakening the importance of heeding these messages. We also acknowledge the difficulties that Starseeds are facing as Earth is reaching a crescendo of duality — darkness is continuously clashing with light as those who feel their grip on power and corruption through a reign of terror and fear slip away as the shift of consciousness towards the light continues around the globe.

Even though the reins of power seem to be in the grip of those intent on serving their own interests, the silent and powerful work of Lightworkers around the world, in communion with the Masters of Light, are making a steady impact on the grip that Third Dimensional energy has had on the human race for so long. It is evident in the way that acts of terror are no longer being tolerated and suffered in silence by groups and individuals who have, up until recently, felt powerless to rise above the domination of authoritarian rule. It is also shown in the noticeable rise in the number of people who are seeking answers to their own existence and higher truths away from the restrictions of religion. The second coming is truly underway.

Now is not the time to shrink in fear. It is time to speak out about the injustices of the world and to reclaim the Mastery that is rightfully yours. All of you upon the Earth have the knowledge of the universe within your grasp as it resides in your Higher Self that is directly linked to the Divine Source. You also all have the ability to create and manifest whatever it is you desire because you all contain the God-seed of Creation which links you directly to the Creator. When you access the Divine knowledge that is your birthright anything is possible. Be warned, however, that what you manifest will directly affect your health and well-being as a matter-of-course — if you manifest for your highest and best and for the greater good, you will reap the benefits in generous and positive ways. However, if what you desire is of benefit to you at the expense of the free-will and health of others, then your rewards will be tarred with the same brush. No-one can expect good fortune and abundance to last when their intentions are self-serving, destructive and against spiritual law. The benefits may at first seem glorious, but there is always a consequence for choosing the darker road.

There are many ways that ordinary humans can make a difference to living conditions upon the Earth. You may feel insignificant and powerless against the force of so much evil, but it is timely to remind you all that anything that happens on Earth in duality is merely an illusion. In the energy of the Creator, which is unconditional and therefore not ruled by duality, all is one and only love is real. Nothing else exists. The drama of duality is all consuming and never-ending — when you are caught in its trap there seems to be no way out with only bleakness and darkness ahead. However, if you reconnect to the light of Creator your focus will shift and so will your vantage point. This will allow you to see that anything manifested in the energy of unconditional love can have no other returns. This is the energy in which all humans must strive to be operating from now on. It is the only way the Earth can escape the clutches of war, violence, hatred and self-destruction.

Religion has taught man that he is separate from God and subservient to Him. Man reveres God and Christ and looks to them to pave the way forward. Their belief is that all of Creation lies in God's hands. Christians wait for the return of Christ and Muslims chant their prayers to Allah, asking for mercy and Divine wisdom. Extremist rebels slay innocent people in the name of Allah. There is no religion in the world today that teaches oneness. All religions are therefore disempowering to the human spirit because they look to serve as a medium between people and God. Many people feel that the only way to be in touch with God is in a church. Worse still, most humans feel they are sinners and not worthy to ask anything of God, let alone be His equal.

The world of duality is built upon inequality. Subservience, powerlessness, helplessness and the unequal sharing of wealth are the reality lived by humans every day. But, in the energy of the Creator, the human being is an equal co-creator who can change his/her reality simply through changing their belief system. What you believe you will create; what you create will be your reality if you accept it to be so. Change your beliefs and you can change your reality. If you believe in oneness you immediately empower yourself with the unconditional love of the Creator, and more importantly, with the resources of the universe at your fingertips. It is that simple.

There are many healing modalities upon the Earth at this time, some of which deal only with the physical body. Others use holistic methods that treat all four bodies: physical, emotional, mental and spiritual. Many people now meditate as a matter of course, and the quest to connect to one's own spirituality has never been more prevalent or more urgent. It is time to reconnect with your God-Self, the Creator within who is spiritually aware of themselves and is always connected to Source.

Become aware of yourself as a being of energy. In fact, everything that exists in the universe is made of matter that consists of particles that move and, as they move, they expend energy. Your body, then, is made of cells that are renewing all the time as energy is spent and tissue is worn-out. To replenish and renew your cells you must consume energy in the form of food that is nourishing to your body. However, the human body consists of four bodies, all of which require the consumption of energy in order to expend it. Physical exhaustion is well known, but mental and emotional exhaustion are just as common and are a result of unequal exchanges of energy, which in turn, cause a depletion of resources and an inability to function. Spiritual exhaustion is also possible through a person's feelings of rejection, disconnection and of being unloved. Feelings and emotions equate to energy, and if a human's feelings and emotions are hurt, betrayed or suffering trauma, the energy exchange will be out of balance and an actual physical illness could occur.

It is easy to see how a person can become out of balance if all four bodies are not nourished and cared for. Within the spiritual, or causal, body lie energy wheels called 'chakras'. These energy centres are vortex points for the person's energy exchange, and if they are blocked or out of balance equal exchanges of energy will not be able to occur. There are seven major chakras, yes, but there are over three hundred chakras in the body that require certain frequencies of light to flow through them. The human body is, indeed, a marvellous structure, but the fact that all humans evolve from the light of creation means that the complexity of energy is far beyond just physical realities.

It is necessary, now more than ever, to begin to raise the frequencies of light in your chakras to allow your Lightbody* to once more enter your spiritual body. When your Lightbody is fully activated you will know a higher way of thinking and being that will take you out of the drama of the Third Dimension. You will be aligned to the Crystalline Grid** and to Mother Earth's diamond core, as well as being totally in harmony with your divine, God-self. Raising your energies to the Fifth Dimension through your chakras is essential to achieving ascension and oneness.

While there are many practitioners who can help you to bring in your Lightbody, merely holding the intention and asking for help and guidance is enough to begin the process. Permission is essential, for neither we in the angelic kingdom, nor the creator Himself, can intervene until you have asked. We can then begin to assist you to clear, align and balance your energy centres so that higher frequencies of light can come in. Bringing your four bodies into a higher state is not without its side-effects, and when the process has begun you may experience periods of nausea, dizziness and disequilibrium. You may also feel tremors and strange vibrations in different parts of your body, but all of these experiences are normal and not harmful. We urge you to persist, for the results of bringing in your Lightbody will be of benefit to you, those around you and to the planet herself.

Universal energy comes in all forms and in many levels of vibration. All seven planes of existence will provide healing and advice to the person who asks for it, but there will be demands upon the inquirer because of the conditions for accessing the knowledge and healing energy from that plane. Only the Seventh Plane, or the Creator of All That Is, contains no conditions and protects, rather than drains, a person's energy. The sphere of light that is the Creator's essence is said to be above all the other Planes of Existence, when in fact it encompasses them and is an integral part of them. They are layers of vibration that make up a whole. The complexity of the six other planes can make the simplicity of the Seventh Plane deceivingly simple, but the truth is that the Seventh Plane contains the essence of unconditional love that binds all of the other planes together. The lack of vows and commitments in the Seventh Plane makes it the only plane where transfers and trading of energy, resulting in such things as fatigue, illness and illusions of grandeur, do not occur. It is the plane where all is one and there is no duality. Everything just is. It is only possible to work with the lower planes and to not be bound by the vows and commitments of them when you first connect to the light and love of the Seventh. Then you will be protected from absorbing other people's negative energies and from jeopardising your health and well-being.***

You are one with the Creator and a co-creator of the universe. There are no requirements for you to be loved by Him because you and He are one and the same. When you can feel with all of your bodies and connect to your spirituality, your God-self, you will begin to work in his light and move away from the illusion of duality. Work from and with the light and you will vibrate at a much higher frequency that will attract people, situations and fortunes of the same or even higher vibrations. You alone have the power to change the world by changing your vibrations by bringing in the light of the Creator and sending it out to the world.

And so it is.

* For more information on the lightbody see
"Raising the Energies of Mother Earth Towards Ascension 2012: The Highest Truth." (Cochrane, 2013, Balboa Press).

** See *Chapter 9*

*** For more information of the Planes of Existence see
Stibal, V. (2006). Theta Healing. Idaho, U.S.A. Rolling Thunder Press.

CHAPTER 6
The Universal Mind

The universe seems unlimited, both in its size and its potential. There is much unexplored territory, and so little is known to the human mind. However, if you put aside your human mind, which is limited in its belief systems and its knowledge, and think with your universal mind, you will be astonished at what you know to be true and what you comprehend when you previously did not.

The universal, collective consciousness unites all beings on Earth. Every thought goes into the universal, collective consciousness and creates either negativity or positivity. This consciousness affects the status quo on Earth and can be either awakening or damaging. The universal consciousness connects the human minds of all persons on Earth and also connects to the universal mind which holds the knowledge of the universe. This knowledge is available to any ethereal being who is willing to avail themselves of this knowledge and who is also willing to share it. Not all beings in their ethereal state are ready to learn or evolve, and so not all avail themselves of universal knowledge between lives. The higher soul, however, will have a thirst for knowledge and will wish to learn and to grow. Higher souls are continually in service, so they do not wish to keep knowledge to themselves. They will either reincarnate in order to teach others in the human state, or they will attempt to transmit this knowledge to both ethereal beings and those in human form from the ethereal plane.

The universal mind is different to the universal human collective consciousness and is also available to all humans. This ethereal consciousness is forever transmitting universal knowledge and wisdom to those who are willing or able to listen. It may come in the form of intuition or as a toning or whistling sound. It may be a dream, a thought or just an inner knowing. It will also be transmitted when asked directly asked for in meditation. The knowledge of the universe in the universal mind encompasses all living planets and their inhabitants from the past, present and future.

The universal mind is at one with God's mind, but the difference is that the universal mind is static, a data bank if you will, while God's mind is a living, breathing thing of creation. God's mind is constantly using knowledge to create based on decisions already made and new knowledge being learned. When universal knowledge is accessed from the universal mind in conjunction with

God's mind, which is the basic intention to create, powerful manifestations will occur. However, one must be very careful of one's intentions, as the deliberate intent to do harm or evil will have dire consequences, not just for the intended victim/s, but also for the perpetrator.

In search of universal wisdom you must ask yourself: Why do you wish to know it? What are your intentions with this sacred knowledge? If your intentions are to assist those on Earth to ascend, or to raise Mother Earth out of Third Dimensional energy, then your reward will be to live in the light and to evolve towards Mastery. If, however, your intentions are to harm your planet and those who live upon it, your reward will be to live in darkness, at least until you learn that such a road can benefit no-one, let alone be sustained.

One way to access the universal mind is to access your higher self through your sacred heart. You must clear your mind of all thoughts, and you must also believe that you can receive these messages. Your higher self is your direct access to the universal mind, while your Sacred Heart is your direct connection to God's mind. Connect to your higher self through your sacred heart. You will be surprised at what you know that you previously had no knowledge of! Ask your question or hold your intention while centring your energy in your heartspace. Bring your higher self into your heartspace and completely clear your mind. Meditate on the question and the knowing will come. It may take practice, but you will find that the answer will become clearer over time. Other ways to access the universal mind is through contact with the Masters of Light or members of the Inter-Planetary Galactic Federation. When meditating, specifically ask for guidance from whomever you most trust to answer your questions and to lead you to the wisest cause of action. There are also many different channels of universal knowledge that can be accessed from planets across the universe, and some of these are described in later chapters of this book.

The accessing of the universal mind depends upon a person's integrity and the ability to trust — in themselves, in their ability to access the information and in the reliability of the information they are receiving. If you do not trust, then the information received could be compromised or even untrustworthy. Always ask to receive information, healing or manifestations for your highest and best, and give thanks and gratitude for everything that is given to you, no matter how small. It is in the nature of the receiving that will influence the integrity and vibration of the gift.

Lightworkers and Wayshowers all over the world and, indeed, across the universe, are now being called upon to access the data bank of the universal mind and to use this sacred knowledge, in conjunction with God's mind, to assist the Earth to heal and to ascend. We, the Masters of Light and members of the Inter-Planetary Galactic Council are here to assist you in this quest. There is no deed too small that cannot make a difference to the energy and vibratory patterns on Earth at this time. Work in the light and you will attract abundance and love. Work in the darkness and you will invoke great karma on yourself that will take many lifetimes to repay. All paths lead to the light, and all light energy comes from the Creator, yet the choices you make in terms of the paths you choose will determine the length of your journey.

And so it is.

CHAPTER 7
Traversing Time and Space

It has long been the dream of mankind to travel through space and, to a large degree, that dream has been realised. However, the ability to traverse beyond Earth's solar system is not possible for the human in physical form, and will only ever remain a dream. Space travel for other planets and beings, however, is a reality that transcends human knowledge, understanding and scientific/technological capabilities and have enabled aliens from many other planets to visit, and even live upon, the Earth.

Travelling through time and space through portals is not a new concept: the universe does not operate in time; in fact, time does not exist in the universe other than on planet Earth. Time is a mechanism for humans to keep track of their history, but, in reality there is only this present moment. In this way, time portals are not really such. They are more space portals, for when you use them you may be traversing large distances in an instant without time being a factor.

There are many time portals surrounding the planet Earth that potentially link to other parts of Earth and to other worlds and they diminish time and space as humans know it. Time portals are only one means of transporting one's energy to another time and place. They are openings that allow one to be in another place or time instantly and are not place-specific; this means that they are simply a means of moving to any place by using clear intent. Any portal can be used to go, and any other can be used to return. As long as you clearly state where it is you are sending your consciousness you will always arrive at your destination.

There may be instances when one needs to go back in time on the Earthly Plane to send healing or to view an occurrence in a past life. A time portal may be used, but one can also use the timeline which will take you to any past or future event. Using the timeline is not wise, however, if one has not had tuition in how to use it, as going anywhere above your consciousness can be dangerous if you have had no experience in such matters.

To traverse time or space using one of these portals or the timeline it is necessary to raise your consciousness in a meditative state. It is not yet possible for humans to use a time portal in their physical body, although this may become a reality in the future. At present one can visit other places and worlds through several means in meditation if one is knowledgeable about such things. There are no places off limits, as long as one stays within the boundaries of spiritual law and does not impinge upon any other's free will, including those beings on other planets or in other dimensions.

When you take your consciousness out of your body you must be careful to be in full awareness of where it is and of how to get back. You must always protect yourself by grounding your energy before you go, using full awareness and intent of where you are sending your energies, and re-grounding yourself once you return. You should also always be totally aware of whom it is you are channelling and meeting. If you are not, you leave your energy open to attack by lower energies.

The ability to send one's consciousness out of one's body to traverse time and distance in a meditative state is known widely as remote viewing. This is also not a new concept, and is an exceptional ability to have if one is an Earth healer and is using the ability to help the planet and its people. However, it is an ability that could be potentially intrusive and used for personal gain which, of course, would be against spiritual law. With ability comes great responsibility which is not to be taken lightly. The degrees to which one could assist the planet with the use of remote viewing increase with the positiveness of the intent. The possibilities for great harm are also increased in the wrong hands. One should never use space portals, the time line or any type of remote viewing for any other purpose than to assist Mother Earth or to send energy and healing to those in need. To do otherwise would be against spiritual law and would immediately invoke the law of karma against the perpetrator.

Human beings associate alien visits with spaceships and, in many cases, this is the case. However, beings from all other planets have used space portals and teleportation arbitrarily to traverse the universe for centuries, and many aliens walk amongst you unnoticed today through these means of travel. Their visits are entirely peaceful and are intended as merely observational — they are gathering data on the rate of ascension amongst humans and on the state of the human consciousness. They do not intervene in any way, although they would gladly help if asked. For instance, there is a population of shape-shifters called the Shadow People who form their own planet by merely joining together. They are a consciousness that do not need a physical body to exist, and they exist in peace and love and in harmony with each other and the universe. They travel through space as easily as fish move through water and many times faster. They do not consume energy nor do they give out any toxins. They are not living as such but their consciousness is of essence and very intelligent. They have been heard and even seen by some on Earth as they come in briefly to observe our ways and to educate their younger 'offspring', who are really just threads of the main Shadow People thought-stream. They are able to traverse galaxies and great distances faster than the speed of light, in fact, faster than the speed of thought.

There are several races living upon Earth at this time, humans being one of them. There is also an unfriendly race of Reptilians whose main aim is to gain power and control over others. In many ways they have achieved this aim, but their existence has been detected and many have either left or retreated in an attempt to regroup and attack at a later time. Their methods of attack are insidious and mind-altering, and many walk amongst you as famous or wealthy people. It is a takeover that has been many years in the planning yet always doomed to fail. Their immediate success has invoked much egotistical and invasive behaviour, but the vibration is too low to attain an ascended state. These aliens will suffer the consequences of their actions for many lifetimes to come, but all roads lead to the light eventually.

Other races represented on your Earth at this time include Arcturuns, Siriuns, Orionions and Pleadians. Many of them have actually reincarnated as humans, which is the easiest way to inhabit Earth, but it can also bring with it its own problems, such as the memories of life on their home planet which do not resonate with the vibrational patterns on Earth. As a result, many of the early deaths of humans being witnessed on Earth are actually reincarnated aliens who have not been able to assimilate the dense living vibrations of Earth, even in a human body. Equally and in the same way, other early and 'untimely' deaths are reincarnated Masters of Light who find the density of thinking and harshness of ego too difficult to handle for the length of a human lifetime. Either way, their decision to depart is entirely theirs to make and the lessons they take with them will still be of value to those who receive their help in the ethereal kingdoms.

Aliens are bound by spiritual law as equally as humans and souls who have passed into the ethereal kingdoms are. For a spirit to inhabit a living body is a travesty against humans or aliens and is strictly prohibited under spiritual law. If beings from other planets wish to visit Earth in order to study humans, they must do so in ways that does not contravene anyone's free will. Equally, humans must abide by the same laws in the discovery and treatment of alien visitation.

The ability to traverse the universe at the speed of light and through space portals has been known and used by beings from other worlds for many centuries, and the technologies far outweigh anything that human beings have been able to invent or produce. However, there are some alien travel technologies that have been written of and even broadcast as fiction on Earth that are, in fact, a reality. If humans knew how to use them, would they wish to create alliances with the worlds from whence they came or would they become invaders and terrorists for power and financial gain? This is a question that the Inter-Planetary Galactic Federation asks themselves often. They are willing to help Earth to gain ascension and to live peacefully, yet they are well aware of the dangers behind human ego and the lure of the power that could be gained over other worlds in the universe by Earth with the attainment of alien technologies. They are not blind, nor ignorant, to the foibles and weaknesses of Third Dimensional human energies.

It is not intended, at this time, that humans be assisted to physically visit other planets through alien technologies. However, there are many Lightworkers and Wayshowers who have been shown alien ways of life through remote viewing and meditation, and their understandings will be important in the future for building relationships and breaking down barriers of fear and negativity in the wider, global community.

Humans cannot afford to reject the help of other races who have already learnt the lessons of ego and who have achieved a Fifth Dimensional state. There is much to be gained through peaceful alliances with other planets, but it must be done in an energy of exchange, not exploitation. In embracing the help and knowledge that these planets offer you, not for personal gain or power, but for the good of all, humans will form an important bridge between Earth and alien planets that will only lead to enhanced relationships and the development of peace and goodwill across the universe.

And so it is.

CHAPTER 8
The War on the Astral Plane

The world as humans know it is really an illusion — it is the Third Plane of existence and is the dimension in which humans experience physical form. It appears to be removed from the ethereal world but this is not the case. Humans generally describe three dimensions within their realm of reality: Earth, Heaven and Hell. There are, however, seven planes of existence* which exist in conjunction with each other, but within each of these planes, in particular the Fourth, Fifth and Sixth, there can be hundreds of degrees of vibration within each plane. Humans interact with all planes of existence within the Third Dimension of Earth. When you walk upon the soil, dig for gold, climb mountains or take minerals you are interacting with the First Plane of Existence. When you use herbs in your cooking, make a vegetable garden or take vitamins you are working within the Second Plane of Existence. The Third Plane, or Third Dimension, is the one where you experience life in a physical body and all of the emotions that come with having an ego.

The Fourth Plane is that of the spirit world and where all human spirits go when the physical body has died. This dimension is like Earth but is vibrating at a higher frequency — each person's spirit will maintain the physical appearance it held in life and will continue to learn and evolve as a living consciousness. There are many levels to the Fourth Plane, and the vibration in which the person lived will be reflected in its spirit. Lower, less-evolved spirits reside in the lower levels of the Fourth Dimension and living humans would do well to leave this area of the spirit world well alone. Reiki, Tarot card readings, Shamans, Witch Doctors and Mystics all access the Fourth Plane for healing and wisdom, which can be very powerful but can also come with a trading of energy or inflation of ego, often darkening the energy of the healing. Ghosts reside between the Third and Fourth Planes — they have not passed over to the spirit world yet their physical bodies are no longer alive. Their vibrations are higher than that on Earth yet lower than the Fourth Plane, which is why they can sometimes be seen or heard. Trapped spirits may need help to release to the light, but if they refuse to go they can be commanded to go in Jesus' name. The Astral Plane is between the Fourth and Lower Fifth Planes and is a place where humans send their consciousness to in their sleep to meet their guides and soul mates. It is also the place that collects human and spiritual energy, and the residual energy can be extremely negative. This is also the place where the battle between good and evil really begins.

The Fifth Plane or Dimension is in two main degrees — the Lower and Upper Fifth Planes. The Lower Fifth Plane is an extension of the spirit world and holds lower angelic energies who have not yet resolved their lessons. Witchcraft and Voodoo can be accessed from this dimension, and any healing or karmic act invoked from beings within it will bring swift and dire consequences for both perpetrators and recipients. Curses and demonic energies can be manifested from the Lower Fifth Plane, but will only become a reality if they are invested in by the believer. The Upper Fifth Plane is the Angelic Realm and is the plane that could be most associated to Heaven. The Masters of Light, the Temples of Light, the Hierarchy of angels and archangels and the Angels' Garden are all here on the Upper Fifth Plane. This is the plane where the war between good and evil rages, and all beings from this plane, as loving as they are, will always have the Greater Good in the forefront of their intentions. Anyone working from this plane for healings and readings may find themselves caught in the battle with the Dark Forces and may become entangled in the spirit world as well.

The Sixth Plane is where the Akashic Records of all human lives is kept. It is also the dimension of the Universal, or Spiritual, Laws. If you work with astrology, numerology, tones, sacred geometry, pendulums or runes, or if you go back to view a past life, you are accessing the Sixth Plane of Existence.

The Seventh Plane of Existence is the light of the Creator of All That Is. When you enter this plane you will see no people and no colours. It is the plane of unconditional love and the highest truth. This is the only plane where there are no conditions on healings, readings or any type of interaction with living or non-living things. Everything just is. All of the other planes have their own vows and commitments that are immediately, if not consciously, subscribed to as soon as its energy is accessed by the human. Many of these vows and commitments demand an exchange of energy that can physically, mentally, emotionally and even spiritually drain the person using the energy. It can also behold the person to its commitments and force him/her to stay bound to that plane. The only way to avoid being bound by any of the lower six planes' vows is to at first connect with the Creator of All That Is in the Seventh Plane.

In the fight for ascension, dark and light forces have been battling it out for centuries on the Astral Plane but, in reality, the war has already been won and the ascension of the Earth has occurred. The term 'Dark Forces' refers to anyone who wishes to control the Earth for their own selfish gains, and not all who subscribe to their beliefs are human. Many of those working in liaison with them are of ethereal nature and of an extremely low, Fourth Plane vibration. Their egos, whether human or in spirit, are inflated to such a degree that their own selfish needs are overwhelming and the desire to control and manipulate for power and financial gain is the driving force. The darkness of the spiritual forces cannot be underestimated, and their control over the minds of their human counterparts is absolute. They will stop at nothing to keep the world in the Third Dimension, and many global events can be attributed to their interference, including those blamed on terrorism. The world's media are also being controlled and, for the large part, humans are being duped and led to the slaughter. Mind control works on fear, and most of the Western population have fallen into the trap.

The Angelic Realm have been fighting the Dark Forces for centuries now. The turmoil on Earth which has seen severe disruptions in weather patterns, natural disasters and a prevalence of terrorist attacks is largely due to intervention from those who are desperate to keep control of human minds. Humans, however, are waking up and are uniting in the face of destruction. Anger is overtaking fear, and this powerful emotion is causing many people to fight back. The resilience of the human heart will be, and actually has been, the saving grace of the world.

In the energy of the Creator, the Seventh Plane of Existence, the war on the Astral Plane is all an illusion because duality does not exist. In the Seventh Plane everything that exists in the universe is part of the all and is therefore united as one. All humans are an integral part of the Divine, and as such are one with God and with each other. The illusion of the Third Dimension is that everyone and everything is separate. It is a dangerous illusion that causes much heartache, disconnection, persecution, poverty and segregation on Earth.

Be mindful that most of the information that being fed to you through the media is propaganda and sensationalised to keep you all in fear. Do not engage in the dramas that are feeding the lower emotions of hatred and revenge, because this will only perpetuate and elongate the misery that it is all causing. Connecting to the higher energy of the Creator will allow you to see all that is occurring from a higher perspective and to disengage your energies and emotions from it. Send love, dear ones, and remember that all that occurs on the stage of Earth is a lesson towards soul evolvement and spiritual growth. Work on raising your vibrations above the Third Dimension and radiate the love and light of the Creator out to the world and beyond. The effects on the vibrations of the Earth cannot be underestimated.

And so it is.

CHAPTER 9
The Crystalline Grid

The Crystalline Grid is the Lightworker's grid that encircles the world. Its diamond points criss-cross the Earth creating vortexes of energy that link in with ley lines and energy points on the planet. Mother Earth's diamond core is the anchor for the grid and is the mirror image of each vortex point.

The Lightworker's grid is the access point for each Lightworker on Earth to hold and channel energy for Mother Earth as she continues to consolidate her ascension. It beams down light to her continuously, breaking the patterns of darkness that relentlessly emit negative energy. It links directly in the Universal Human Collective Consciousness, spreading positivity and love into a never-ending supply of negative energy that streams up from global human consciousness. People who have anchored their energy into the grid are directly and always connected to the Creator, the angelic realms, Mother Earth, Her diamond core and to each other. The grid is a place for communication, telepathy and manifestation. It is also a powerful place for healing — both for sending it and receiving it.

The core of Mother Earth is a 12 pointed diamond, and each point itself has twelve points. This core holds Mother Earth's heart, and is susceptible to the negative energies reverberating through her. There was a time when her diamond core was weak and cracking — her heart was literally breaking and in the depths of despair. However, since her alignment with the Crystalline Grid and with the hearts and minds of Lightworkers around the world, her heart beats strongly once again. Those who have been to her core in meditation will know how strongly she loves and how susceptible to the pain and torment of humans she is. She greatly appreciates the continued work of those who send her light, love and the Violet Flame of Transmutation* daily, and cannot express enough how powerful this positive energy is for the health of the planet and of the human race.

The Crystalline Grid is not new, but it is not ancient either. It has only been in place since around the turn of the 21st century and is a replacement for older, more traditional grids, including ley lines that previously protected the Earth's energy. Many traditional owners of the land held the energy in the previous grid, and this energy has now dispersed into the Crystalline Grid, bringing with it the energy of oneness and ascension. Those who hold their energy in the Crystalline

Grid are able to feel their connection at any time, and their intention to send healing energy to the Earth, no matter where or when they are directing their consciousness, will send the energy through the grid, therefore connecting it to Divine and Angelic energy. This magnification of energy sent to the Earth or to other humans is an extremely powerful source, and the impact can only benefit the Earth and mankind itself.

Every human holds a vortex of energy on the Earth. The energies they hold and emit to others and the world at large is either negative or positive, and will attract negative or positive energy accordingly. When people become conscious of their selves in spirit and of their own light, they become powerful Lightworkers who are capable of spreading light and love with purposeful intent. If they consciously connect their energy to the Crystalline Grid the vortex of energy that they hold becomes more powerful still and the healing effects on the planet cannot be overestimated.

The Crystalline Grid connects Lightworkers around the world in a way that has never been achieved before. When individual Lightworkers who are connected to the grid send love and light to the Earth they immediately harness the energy of every other Lightworker on the grid, as well as the power of Divine love and angelic light. In this way, the Crystalline Grid has harnessed the power of the Law of Group Endeavour and has become a powerful force against the dark forces who continue to attempt to keep the Earth in fear and despair. The simple act of loving another human being unconditionally for who they are sends enough light to raise the vibrations of the world one more notch above the darkness and one step closer to ascension. The power of love can never be underestimated and is the single emotion that is capable of saving the world from being forever plunged in the Third Dimension.

The energy that pulsates through the Grid is capable of healing anyone who holds their energy there. It is also the place where Lightworkers can recharge or receive upgraded energy and updated downloads to help them to continue on their own ascension path. The light on the Grid is ethereal, Divine light that is impervious to lower energies. The more Lightworkers who connect consciously to the Grid the higher the vibrations on Earth and in the surrounding Universal Consciousness.

The vibrations on Earth continue to rise despite the many tragedies and calamitous events that strike on a daily basis. With each major tragedy, which threatens to plunge affected survivors and indeed, the world, into eternal grief and despair there come many blessings. The unification of the world in love, tolerance and understanding will come when people stand up against violence, terrorism and attacks against the rights of everyone on Earth to live as they wish according to the Law of Free Will. The war has already been won — Ascension has already been achieved. The only way to bring the energy of human consciousness into the Fifth Dimension is through the energy of the Creator which defies dualism and unites the human race with the rest of the universe as one.

One does not need to be labelled a 'Lightworker' in order to send healing to Mother Earth's diamond core or to harness the Violet Flame's magical energy. One merely needs to hold the intent of sending love, light and healing anywhere in the world or to anyone in particular and it will be done. To access the Crystalline Grid, however, one must at first become a crystalline energy oneself, as the energy of the Grid is powerful and can cause a person to feel sick and unbalanced if their energies have not been raised enough to cope with the higher frequencies of light. The Lightbody, or your Crystalline Body, can be activated within your cells by Masters of Light. Before they can activate your chakras to higher vibrations you must work to keep your energies as high and as unblocked as possible. Raise your conscious awareness to the health of your body and mind and connect to your spirituality through meditation, grounding and gentle healing practices. The more you work to clear your body and mind of toxic thoughts, emotions, past trauma, food and unhealthy influences the readier you will be to accept the higher frequencies of ascension.

Fear divides where love unites. There is no other way to rid the Earth of hatred, fear, despair, terrorism and war other than loving one another despite any differences you may have and to work on one's own self. God does not judge, as he has given the Earth to all humans as the stage to learn your lessons towards soul growth, mastery and enlightenment. He loves you and holds you in His light, willing you all to see that His love and light are available to you free from religious bias and doctrine. The word of God is love; that is all there is. The more each person on Earth can harness His love by bringing His light into their energy fields and into their conscious state, the less people will submit to the doctrines of fear and separatism that are lowering the vibrations of the world and keeping them in the Third Dimension.

Ask for help in this quest, and it will be given. We are ever with you.

And so it is.

* To read about the Violet Flame of Transmutation refer to *"Raising the Energies of Mother Earth Towards and After Ascension 2012: The Highest Truth" (Cochrane, 2013).*

PART 2
The Inter-Planetary Galactic Federation

CHAPTER 10
The Inter-Planetary Galactic Federation

The universe is ablaze with light and colour. The vastness of the territory masks the plethora of life that abounds within the galaxies and solar systems. The Inter-Planetary Galactic Federation (IPGF) is a body that represents five galaxies, the one you call the 'Milky Way' being one of those. Each galaxy has a different number of solar systems and planets sustaining life within them. There are nine solar systems in your galaxy with eight suns and nine planets that sustain life. The universe is extremely vast, and each member of the IPGF representing their planet has a wide area to traverse in order to maintain communications with each other.

Little is known of the IPGF on Earth or even of its existence. It is necessary for such a federation to exist so as to monitor the inter-planetary interactions that occur as a matter of course. The federation also has jurisdiction over all precincts in the universe, and is the governing body overseeing all affairs to do with inter-planetary decisions and business agreements. Each solar system has an average of seven representatives, depending on the number of inhabited planets within them, but some have as little as two and as many as ten. In all, there are currently 32 planets represented in the IPGF. There are no elections, only rotations, and each member is welcomed and treated with respect and dignity.

Each planet has its own governance that is voluntary and works on a rotational basis. All members of a planet's community is eligible to serve on its High Council and in turn, members of the High Council can then nominate to represent their planet on the Inter Planetary Galactic Federation. Representation is for seven Earth years, although time is not measured as such in other solar systems and galaxies. Members of the IPGF are usually older and more experienced High Council members, but this is not always the case — as all community members from each planet is considered equal, all participation is voluntary and non-discriminatory.

Earth, of course, is currently unrepresented on the IPGF council. There are five other planets that are outside the IPGF's jurisdiction because they have no High Council and their beings are not advanced races. They are peaceful and keep to themselves. A sixth race, Reptilia, is not peaceful and is therefore not included. All in all, the inhabitants of the universe interact through the IPGF and this has largely been peaceable and successful, with a few exceptions. Because each galaxy is so vast and the distances needed to travel are so immense, meetings are conducted in various ways and at different times to suit all members.

The methods of travel for members of the IPGF vary according to purpose and mission and the urgency of the request or demand from planetary high councils. There are roving ships, called Space Wanderers that are manned by volunteers; they travel at the speed of light and can traverse great distances in seconds. Space Wanderers use wormholes and time-tunnels to travel through to different dimensions, galaxies and solar systems. There are also mother ships that stay in space to refuel space wanderers and passing traffic. The IPGF meets on these ships as a central meeting point. Other forms of travel for communication purposes are remote viewing, teleportation and astral travelling.

The IPGF has many duties including the overseeing of interplanetary High Council dealings that oversee trade, the exchange of resources and monitoring of space highway traffic. It also upholds spiritual law and is the body that holds all planets to account. There have not been many transgressions in recent history, but in the distant past there were several events that required firm and decisive action. There are no jails or detention centres on the planets represented by the IPGF, but there are still consequences for those that transgress spiritual law or who attempt to exploit the wealth or good will of a planet and its community. All transgressions or serious omissions of law in dealings are considered fairly, equitably and peacefully. It is not often that transgressions against spiritual or planetary law are deliberate, but it can occur.

The IPGF currently have no jurisdiction over Earth or its solar system. This is not to say that they do not monitor its energies and frequencies, as any shift or disturbance has consequences for the energies and frequencies in the entire universe. This must be made clear to all on Earth. No decision humans make and no action you take, however small, is confined to the boundaries of your planet or solar system, as the energies radiate out and are felt on other planets, solar systems and even in other galaxies. Humans may believe that aliens are dangerous, but it is the human race who is considered the most dangerous by the Inter-Planetary Galactic Federation because it is unstable and unpredictable in its behaviour patterns. The presence of ego makes the human a formidable opponent, for the human, (speaking globally rather than individually), will typically choose to serve himself rather than the greater good. 'Saving one's own skin' and 'skimming the cream off the top for one's own benefit' are not terms familiar with beings on planets represented by the IPGF. Understandably, they are wary of any encounters with humans and, although they will assist humans if asked, will always be prepared against attack.

The IPGF are a powerful but peaceful body who guard and protect the universe and who control inter-planetary dealings. Their presence should be a comfort to you at this time, because the combined assistance of many planets in the ascension and resurrection of the Earth will greatly accelerate the process and unify the solar systems of the universe. The planets within the Inter-Planetary Galactic Federation all contain intelligent beings who co-exist in harmony and oneness. They mostly live as colonies, although this is not entirely true for the planet Arcturus and a few of the smaller planets in the IPGF's jurisdiction. Their ways of life are much simpler than western life on Earth, yet their forms of communication, transport and technological systems are far superior. The immense distance between planets, solar systems and galaxies means that ways of transportation and communication must be fast and efficient. Space ships are only one way of traversing the universe but they are often not favoured by councils who need to communicate with several planets at once or who need to travel across large distances in a short space of time.

The ascension of the universe has been some time in the making but many years in the passing. All planets supporting life, with the exception of Earth and a scattering of others, achieved oneness and overcame the need for conflict many eons ago. This is due to several factors, one being the superior intellect of alien beings which supersedes the need to serve self. Highly intelligent life forms perceive life or existence as part of a whole. Everything must be in order, because order reduces the chance for mistakes. In an orderly life, where everything runs to plan and all life is respected, everything in existence is equal and all remains in balance. There is no need for inequality or for one sector of the population to be superior to another. Spiritual law underpins all ways of life, and respect is the value shared by all beings in the colony, the community, on the planet, and in the federation.

The existence of life beyond Earth and its solar system is not a mystery to many humans, because the vastness of the universe is a fact and it would be the utmost arrogance to consider that Earth is the only planet to sustain life. There are many humans who are now receiving messages from planets within and beyond your galaxy, and the names of these planets and the life forms that exist on them are becoming more widely known. Many humans have accepted assistance from these beings in the past and written about it, but only a small number of believers have been willing to listen. In contrast, many humans have been interfered with by aliens as a result of unconscionable dealings with trusted government agencies, and these experiences have resulted in fear and distrust of aliens amongst the greater human population. The energies of the past are now shifting and changing, however, as the climate and the vibrations of humans upon the Earth becomes less stable. Many people are looking beyond the solar system for answers to the dire situation the human race finds itself in. It is time now for believers and non-believers alike to open their minds and their hearts to the possibilities that are available to you amongst the stars, should you choose to look, listen and accept.

It is so.

CHAPTER 11
Orion

Orion is a large, white planet with brown and orange stripes. It is in the neighbouring galaxy to the Milky Way and is a sister planet to Earth. In fact, both Sirius and Orion are sister planets to Earth, and there is much communication between the beings on both planets. The ways on Sirius are much the same as on Orion, and their communications are mostly friendly ones. There is no war or hostility between them, but they keep their own jurisdictions and are business-like in their manner when it comes to such matters. There is nothing that cannot be worked out, and there has never been a harsh word spoken between anyone on Orion with those on Sirius. The definition of 'being neighbourly' can be found in the example of the relationship between these two planets.

Sirius is larger and more densely populated than Orion. It holds more resources, which it shares willingly and fairly with Orion and other planets which do not have as much to rely on. Fair exchange between people on Sirius and, indeed, with those on Orion, does not include money or any financial exchange. Energy is exchanged through simple communications, through pleasant words and through honouring each other for the energy given. There is no expectation around financial or material gain in any way on either planet, because no being that lives on either Sirius or Orion has an ego. The greater good and what benefits all is the only agenda on these planets. This is where Earth has the most to learn.

Orion holds much information to help with survival on Earth. The landscape of Orion is vast, empty and barren. This is the natural landscape, but the city of life is situated above it. The people have learned to generate their own food and means for living because their planet does not provide it, and everything they use is recycled and re-used — nothing goes to waste. There is water, and some sparse vegetation, but no animals exist on Orion. There is also some heat and sunlight from their nearest star. The adaptations of Orionions is to live cleanly and without waste, taking little from the planet but giving all back to it. What is taken must be given back for, by just living upon the planet they are taking shelter and safety as their home. For the inhabitants of this planet, Orion is their inspiration to be caretakers, not pillagers, of the land. If Orionions left tomorrow they would leave it as they found it. In that way, their vibration of living is so much higher than that on Earth.

The lessons learned on Orion are available to those who wish to receive this knowledge. Orion, like Earth, is a vast planet with a vast population. Unlike Earth, however, they all speak the same language and have virtually the same customs — they are truly united and one. They do not all look alike, although they have many similarities in their appearances and in their mannerisms — they are individual but they are also similar. All Orionions consider themselves to be part of the large family of Orion.

There is no birth on Orion — they clone from the age of 12, so there are no babies either. This is a deliberate choice, because they feel that the time wasted raising infants is better spent on educating youths in Orionion ways. The DNA of each clone is extracted so that a progression of cloning can be performed at certain intervals as the natural cycles of aging and death occur. There is no 'literacy' on Orion in that they do not learn to read or write. They telepathise their information which is coded numerically. Their knowledge of number systems and mathematics is inbuilt so they do not need to learn it. What they do learn is about the universe and the vast array of solar systems and planetary links. They spend a great amount of their youth learning star charts and intergalactic knowledge. Their computer systems are greatly advanced and are nothing like Earth has ever seen. Their systems are very similar to the way an Orionion brain is coded, which makes internalising information much simpler.

The population of Orion is larger than on Earth, yet their ways of life are much simpler and more peaceful. Because all people are cloned, the family unit does not exist as humans would recognise it. However, whenever cloning is taken place the new, young Orionions are sponsored by inter-generational groups who live in share houses and who raise and educate the young ones in Orionion ways. These groups become families of sorts, but as they grow people move on according to their roles in the community and on planetary councils. There are many roles to play on a planet with such a large population and, as all people on the planet work to the same end, which is largely survival of the species, all roles are considered as equally important as each other. There is no poverty, no inequality and no unemployment on Orion.

As the population is so large on Orion there are several councils that govern the planet. They make up the larger government, so they meet separately and then all converge to share their counsel. Members are elected as on Earth but there is no campaigning for election, because candidates are selected for their credentials, not their enthusiasm. Although Orionions are cloned and therefore very similar, their personalities do differ according to the coded information the being they were cloned from held. The knowledge they possess determines the degree to which they can assist councils to make decisions and run the planet. Those who run for council but who are not elected form a secondary council who assist the primary councils with administration and communications.

Councils meet to ensure that the supply of resources remains equalised and fair. There is no money on Orion and no exchange in terms of goods and services. All is provided, used and replaced. When it comes to the exchange of goods and services inter-galactically, however, there is a barter system in place that works very well. Members of the Primary Council also serve on the Inter-Planetary Galactic Federation. This council meets regularly and in a central place. Communications can be conducted telepathically of course, and by coded message through a central data base. However, they choose to meet in person at conventions once every 12 years, or sooner if there is anything more urgent to discuss.

The plight of humans on Earth has been a major discussion point for many years now. Since the alignment with Earth of the planets that are members of the Inter-Planetary Galactic Federation they have been discussing ways in which they may help Earth without putting their own planets in jeopardy. The tendency of humans to exploit in order to benefit for their own gain is widely known amongst planetary councils, so contact with humans is always approached with a sizeable degree of caution. However, they are also aware that there is a large contingent of human beings who are kind and committed to the resurrection and ascension of the Earth, and they are keen to communicate with them in order to assist Mother Earth in its ascension process.

Orion is a sister planet to Earth because many humans have lived lives on Orion or were even born there. There is so much of life on Orion that is foreign to Earth, but much of it is known in the human consciousness because of the vast amount of experiences many humans have had there in previous lives. It is now time to access that consciousness and to hear what your sisters and brothers are calling out to you. Hear their wisdom and use it to turn your planet around for the good of all.

Earth has a major advantage in the universe because it is free from restrictions in many ways. The Earth has an abundant supply of resources, there are many less humans on Earth than there are on Orion with a larger area to live upon, there is, to a degree, more freedom of movement, and humans have the advantage of living on and being in touch with the Earth itself. The disadvantages of living on Earth are also many — climate being one and the ego of man himself being another. Man, unlike Orionions, is at war with himself. This is an unnatural state for an Orionion, as it is for most other inter-galactic beings. Man also, for the most part, does not respect his planet or live sustainably — there has been a huge amount of plundering of the Earth's natural resources and this fact alone is the cause of so many of the problems humans are now experiencing upon their planet at this time.

If there were but one message the people of Orion could impart to humans it would be this: respect yourself and respect your planet. With respect comes the mindset that everything you say and do must be of integrity and with the purpose of providing and sustaining life. There is no compromise or sacrifice to be made in the vibration of respect. What you use you must replace, what you say you must mean, what you do must come from a place of integrity and service, not just to self but to the greater good for all. You must all exist together, so it is much better to be in a state of peace and harmony rather than in one of aggravation and competition.

The other important message is to love — without restraint and without condition. There is no room for judgement or condemnation when you are coming from a place of love. The absence of love for self immediately brings one's vibration down into a state of disharmony, disconnection and imbalance. When one does not love self it is impossible to love anyone else or to find the state of mind to care for one's thoughts or actions. The greatest problems on Earth are underpinned by a total disconnection from self which, in turn, disconnects many humans from the Creator and all that is truly important. The illusions of life on Earth are important lessons for soul growth, that is true, but the dramas that are attached to these lessons have little importance in the scheme of the universe or in the creation of balance and harmony. Drama brings one's soul into a state of confusion and into ego. It makes one centre on self and its needs and wants rather than remembering that one's existence on Earth is part of a much bigger picture. Drama is illusion and brings with it a feeling of separatism and unrest. Feelings of unworthiness, mistrust and betrayal will always accompany drama, which leads to a downward spiral into the lower vibrations of anger, hatred and revenge. Can you see that, if you were to keep yourself in a state of love, loving yourself and others unconditionally, the actions and reactions associated with drama would not exist on Earth? This is the biggest lesson that accompanies the gift of ego —

putting your own needs aside and remembering your soul's contract to serve for the greater good. People on Orion do not have egos to contend with, but they do love themselves and each other unconditionally because they accept that they are all one with the planet and the higher Source.

Thirdly, live life in the present moment. There is nothing else that exists or that is of any consequence — the past is behind you and the future is to come. Be present in the present, for the decisions you make consciously will affect the next moment. Be grateful for all that you have and live every day as if it were your last, for the gift of life cannot be underestimated.

Orionions live by the above advice and it serves them well. They do not concern themselves with issues that cannot be undone. However, they strive to learn from any mistakes from the past to improve their demeanour and their future. There is nothing they do in life that they do not mean, and they live and interact in ways that bring them abundance and goodwill. A lifetime of love, laughter and happiness awaits those on Earth who can emulate the lifestyle of Orion. Your time on Earth is precious and relatively short. You must use your time wisely to help heal the planet and to assist other humans in the quest to ascend. The universe awaits you and it is always open to you. It provides what you need when you ask clearly and precisely. It is time to connect, to listen, receive, learn and act.

And so it is.

CHAPTER 12
Sirius

Sirius is a blue planet in the same galaxy as Orion. Many of your souls are familiar with it and may even come from it. Many of you began life there and may even return there after your soul journey upon the Earth is complete. Sirius has many masters and many inhabitants, and it is a democracy of the highest order. The Siriuns consider themselves a community, and no one being is more important than the other. All inhabitants upon the planet of Sirius are equal and all consider themselves to be brother or sister. The community of Sirius resembles a city, which is a series of tunnels and rooms all connected above the ground. Although it is basically a colony, there are differences in that the community is divided into large families who co-exist together in different sections of the city. However, all people on Sirius work towards the greater good which involves the production of resources for the whole community, not just individuals or families.

Life on Sirius rarely changes and all community members work towards the greater good of the planet. All have delegated roles which they uphold for the duration of their lives. The government, which is more a community council, rotates its executive, and all beings upon the planet will hold a place on that council at least once in their lifetime. Decisions are made rationally and for the good of all, as there is no ego on Sirius to create friction or competition amongst the species. The Higher Council of Sirius consists of many hundreds of members. They meet weekly to discuss matters of importance for the planet and to hear grievances from community members. These complaints are never directed towards any individual Siriun nor are they ever taken personally. As you can imagine, a planet as large as Sirius, which is run as a whole community and is not divided into territories or countries as on Earth, cannot function without an enormous amount of organisation and communication. Everything is run with clockwork precision, and every Siriun has their role within the community which they take very seriously. Grievances and complaints directed at the High Council mostly concern the breakdown in technologies or functionalities of equipment and resources on the planet — very few complaints concern any transgression outside of spiritual law or planetary dealings by Siriuns themselves. These kinds of transgressions occasionally do occur, mainly from younger Siriuns who are still learning the customs and cultural ways of the planet. There are no jails on Sirius, nor are there any law-enforcement agencies as such. The High Council deals with all matters pertaining to Siriun business and operations, and any transgression is usually dealt with through education, not punishment.

There is no ego on Sirius so no-one strives to have their needs met above others. The love they feel for each other, however, is not expressed in the way that humans would express it. It is more a feeling of oneness and unity that binds all Siriuns together for life. In this way they love, but it is not a physical love, nor is it even expressed in words such as 'love'. It just is. Siriuns do not enter into relationships but they do have children. Again, the raising of children is for the greater good. When children are born they are not infants, as babies cannot be born on Sirius. The breeding of babies was terminated many hundreds of years ago as there was a virus that swept through the colony and infected many females. The progeny died as a result. It seriously affected the race, and since then all children are cloned from the age of seven and raised in group homes as part of a large family. The numbers of clones are restricted to allow for the natural regeneration of the species — as older members of the community die, more members are cloned to keep the numbers of Siriuns living on the planet the same.

Education on Sirius is uniform and complex. Communications between members are primarily through thought processes, telepathy and numeric sequencing. The language of Sirius is one of coded information, gestures and meaningful sensations that are emitted from the heartspace. Because all Siriuns are cloned, they are 'born' with language and knowledge of Siriun culture already embedded into their brains. However, as the universe is changing and inter-plantery interactions and dealings are constantly evolving, there is much new information to learn to ensure the survival and growth of the planet and its people. Education on Sirius teaches the younger generation how to use and recycle resources on the planet. However, the young students also learn how to emit and 'read' code in several dialects and how to adapt it should they need to interpret language from other planets. In this way all Siriuns are multi-lingual and highly adaptive to the vast amount of information that is being transmitted by other planets and that can be captured on sound and light waves around Sirius.

Humans may think that life on Sirius is boring, for there is rarely a deviation from the clockwork operations upon the planet. However this is the very key to the survival of the planet and the reason that it flourishes. Everyone works together in harmony and no one ever goes without. All Siriuns are well-fed, well-clothed and well-housed. They are all content with their lives, feeling useful and connected. Not one being on the planet ever struggles with emotions such as guilt, hatred, self-doubt or loneliness —they are all united and all one.

Siriuns have mastered the art of space travel and they traverse the universe with ease. They explore other galaxies and solar systems in order to learn the most effective way of living on their planet.

They have not learned well from Earth.

Many Siriuns have died at the hands of humans who sought to exploit their knowledge for their own gain, and they are now extremely wary of any communications from Earth. However, they hold no anger or grudge and they can see that the knowledge they possess, if used in the correct manner, will be useful to help Earth to rise above its current dilemmas and to take its place as a world within the universe that is like all others — peaceful, harmonious and united as one.

It is time for the past to be behind humans and Siriuns alike, and for humans on Earth to learn to control their egos. Raising the vibration of all humans to the Fifth Dimension is the only way to become truly aligned with Sirius, Orion and other planets in the Inter-Planetary Galactic Federation. It is also the only way for them to be able to trust that any information they give will be used for the greater good, not for gain or profit, which is the way of many humans on Earth at this time. Siriuns are ready to help, but the opportunity will be lost if Earth cannot learn to live in the vibration of connection, love, unity and the greater good.

Light takes many hundreds or thousands of years to reach the Earth from stars and planets in the galaxy. The idea of man travelling outside of the Earth's solar system is a fantasy beyond reach because of the amount of time it would take, exceeding the life-span expectation of any human-being attempting it. The dream of man to physically visit any planet such as Sirius or Orion will only ever be that, a dream, yet Siriuns regularly visit Earth and other planets as a matter of course. How can that be so?

The answer to that question is multi-faceted and quite complex, but the simplified answer is that Siriuns do not limit their existence to the physical realm. They are masters of their bodies and of the physicality of the body, but they are also masters of the metaphysical and the spiritual realms. Because they communicate telepathically and in code, they can send their energy anywhere in the universe with intent. They are also masters of technology and can use and manipulate space portals, wormholes, and vortexes of light to travel using either just their bodies or vehicles, and they also teleport their energies. They are absolute masters of mind control and numeric sequences. In an ironic contrast, humans are limited in their space travel by science, yet Siriuns use the art of science, metaphysics, chemistry, biology and spiritual connection to travel wherever they need to go with ease.

Of course, Sirius is not the only planet who has mastered the art of space travel — all advanced planets have. The differences between Sirius and Orion are vast, but there are many similarities as well, one being the way they travel and converse. In that way they are leaders in the universe in terms of communications, and their ability to cover vast distances in a very short time frame has led to both planets having many leaders representing them on the Inter-Planetary Galactic Council.

Knowledge is power, and the knowledge that Sirius and the other planets in the Alliance hold is now offered to those on Earth who have the highest and best intentions for Mother Earth. The knowledge will NOT be imparted to anyone whose intentions are for their own monetary gains or egotistical benefits, but only those Wayshowers whose dearest wish is to see the ascension of Mother Earth will be granted this knowledge, and the assistance to disseminate it.

Now is the time. Are you listening?

CHAPTER 13
The Siriun Blue Flame

The Siriun Blue Flame is a vivid, blue, ethereal flame that has the potential to unite worlds and to transmit information between them. It can be sent by the Siriun High Council, or it can be retrieved by a Master of Light or by a human who is connected to a Master of Light. The flame is transcendental and omnipotent in nature — that is, it can be anywhere and everywhere at once and it cannot be tainted nor overused. There is no keeper of the flame as such, nor are there any conditions on its use other than those prescribed by spiritual law. It can traverse the universe and cross galaxies, it can go through time portals and across dimensions. The Siriun Blue Flame is accessible to those who need it and who intend to use the information to improve the living conditions or technologies on their own planet for the greater good.

The Siriun Blue Flame has lain dormant for some time as there has been no call for its power. It has now been accessed and called into action by Lightworkers on Earth and the Siriun High Council. There is so much that Sirius can teach your planet, notwithstanding the aggression it has encountered in previous attempts to assist. The Blue Flame cannot be activated by anyone whose motivations and intentions are for self-service, greed and corruption, therefore the information coming to Earth will be through people whose energies are higher than the Third Dimension. It is time to take note of what you read and what you hear, and discernment is called for, as is discretion. Those who wish to help Earth will use words that ring of truth and integrity while those whose intentions are for profit and self-gain will use words that condemn, belittle and betray those working for the greater good.

The Siriun Blue Flame provides access and links to universal knowledge and wisdom. It guides the seeker to think higher thoughts and to act from the heart rather than the mind. It reaches within universal law and combines it with the highest truth of the Creator. When you access the Blue Flame the knowledge that you seek, even if you are not sure what it is, will come to you. You will begin to see the universe in your mind's eye. A capsule of light will appear, and when you enter into it the knowledge that you need to know will be told to you. The way you use this knowledge will determine whether you will continue to gain access to it or whether it will later be denied to you, as the flame is of the highest vibration and cannot be used by those in lower vibrations and dimensions.

In the Capsule of Wisdom the flame can transport you to other worlds. It can take you to meet with councils and dignitaries from other planets. It may also show you wisdom that can change your life so you may help others. However, be mindful that if you choose to start accessing the knowledge of the universe in this way, you will be expected to use it to improve your planet and to transmit the information that you gain so all can benefit, not just yourself. Also, once you have opened the portal to the universal mind, you will become an open channel to receiving information. This may be welcome, but for the uninitiated or the inexperienced it can be intrusive and overwhelming. Be careful what you wish for, because all is given and the expectation is that the receiver will also give — of their time, energy and the wisdom they have gained.

The time is nigh for the Siriun Blue Flame to be used by people on Earth to improve their chances of survival, growth and ascension into oneness. Be assured that this time will pass, so the urgency of the need for accessing and using universal knowledge cannot be ignored. There are many humans who remain ignorant of the truths of ascension and of the need to raise their spiritual awareness beyond the dramas of the Third Dimension. They allow themselves to be led by doctrine and propaganda, ignoring the call of their souls to release all fear and to trust in the light of the Creator. Now is the time for the Siriun Blue Flame to be used for the greater good on Earth and for the unity of all life in the universe.

CHAPTER 14
Arcturus

Arcturus is in a solar system on the other side of the universe from Sirius and Orion, yet it is in alignment with these planets with Earth in the centre. The solar system in which Arcturus exist contains three suns but two of them are at the other end of the system and are too far away to have an impact on life on the planet. The solar system is itself three times larger in distance than that of Earth's, yet it contains only nine planets within it. Three of these planets contain life, but Arcturus is the only planet where intelligent life exists. There has been some attempt by the Arcturun people to harvest the life on the other two planets, but they have had little success. This is because the conditions on those planets are dissimilar to theirs and the distance between Arcturus and them is also a barrier to making it viable.

The planet Arcturus is one of extremes — in temperature, in capacity to hold resources and in conditions. There are many places on Arcturus that are uninhabitable, and those places have not been visited for many eons now. The places on the planet that can sustain life are over-populated, so there has been a limit on breeding cycles for some time now in an attempt to bring the population under control. The way of life is simple and uncomplicated. The people live in colonies that are similar in structure and that, while they operate as separate communities, are linked by infrastructure and regular interactions.

Communities live upon the ground, as opposed to Orion and Sirius where the colonies reside in structures built above it. The housing is divided into family apartments and the people live together in family units, much the same as on Earth. The difference is that relationships are not strictly monogamous and there can be several partners in one relationship. There may also be children born from different mothers and/or fathers in the relationship that all live together as a family. To Arcturuns this is a natural state and does not cause any animosity between partners and/or families. There is no cloning on Arcturus which is why there are so many births, and the planet is now facing over-population. The government has put restrictions in place on how many children a family may produce over a period of time, but this is yet to impact the population overall.

Arcturuns are a peaceful people who have come far in their ability to reside in oneness and harmony. Although they do not have an ego that pushes them towards self-service, their history is chequered with war and disharmony, both between themselves and other planets. This is because there was a time where different communities considered themselves separate to their neighbouring ones, and this led to arguments and ill-will. However, their current state and way of life is testament to their strength, determination and the hard work they have done on bringing the planet to oneness and peace. Life on Arcturus is similar to Earth in many ways but it is much more peaceful and harmonious —there is now no war and very little conflict, as the planet has embraced oneness and unification as a matter of course. Family groups form communities that work together to make, farm and grow resources that they share amongst themselves and trade with neighbouring communities. All trade is done fairly and on the basis of equitable exchange.

The weather in places that are inhabited vary in extremes and there are times in an Arcturun year when going outside is dangerous and therefore prohibited. There are many underground areas that serve as shelters and community meeting places. There are also underground tunnels that join communities so that interactions can continue throughout extreme weather conditions. Travel on Arcturus varies from community to community, but the favoured form of transport is air scooter. These simple devices run on energy generated from air that pushes the scooter along just above the ground. They are quite fast, safe and efficient for moving around the colony. For further distances members of the Arcturun High Council and representatives of the IPGF use various forms of air travel that include space ships, aircraft and saucers. There are no fossil fuels on Arcturus — all forms of transport are fuelled by air, electricity or water. Many Arcturuns, however, will never experience space travel in their lifetime.

Water is sometimes a problem and is not always readily available. The harsh weather can mean the planet can go for years without rain. The water storage systems on Arcturus are therefore vast and sophisticated, and the people are extremely cautious and efficient with their water usage. There is much recycling and reticulation used on the planet, and advanced filtering systems ensure that all water, whether it be salt or fresh, is able to be used for human consumption. Nothing goes to waste on Arcturus, and the production of fresh food and water are the major industries on the planet.

Education for the young upon the planet is conducted by elders who have much knowledge and wisdom to impart. There are no 'schools' to attend as on Earth, yet the planet's children study in small groups in their communities with an assigned tutor. Youngsters learn how to speak, write and transmit messages in their mother tongue, Arcturun, but are also schooled in universal languages, including English. They also become very skilled in mathematical calculations and science. There is no discrimination between males and females in subjects offered, and all Arcturun children receive education until they are sixteen Earth years of age. After that they are deemed to be adults and capable of contributing to the planet's workforce. The areas they have shown skills in determine the types of jobs they will be offered and trained in.

All adult Arcturuns are employed in the workforce. There is no unemployment and no discrimination — males and females are all considered able to work any job in their area of expertise. Payment is not with money, as on Earth, but in kind. That means that, whatever the industry that an Arcturun is employed in, be it food, water, clothing, science technologies, is the payment they receive. They then trade with other families to ensure that they have everything they need to live. If there is an abundance of resources in the community they conduct trade fairs to exchange goods with other communities.

Entertainment on Arcturus ranges from games to music and some dancing, but they mostly enjoy coming together over food and engaging in debates and number challenges. There is no wine or addictive substances on the planet, which contributes to the people's ability to remain healthy, peaceful and to live fairly long lives. Telepathy is common and can become a game itself — there are many gatherings that have been conducted in complete silence while the participants battle to dominate each other's minds!

The High Council of Arcturus operates as those on other planets. All adults are given the opportunity to represent the planet on the High Council, but, as the planet's population is bigger than other planets in the Federation, not all adults will become a councillor in their lifetime. Each separate community in the colony is represented on the council, which means that there are several thousand members on it at any given time. On Earth this would become a major problem and cause many issues, but on Arcturus it runs smoothly. Discussions are conducted through computers and all voting is done electronically. Decisions are made democratically and all decisions are final, that is, once voted on it is passed and there is no more discussion on the matter.

Arcturuns are not considered to be as sophisticated a race as Siriuns or Orionions, but they are known to be friendly and accommodating people who will always welcome strangers to their tables. Their way of life is not as orderly or structured as on Sirius and Orion, yet their minds are intelligent and their technologies far more sophisticated than on Earth. In business they are shrewd but not cutthroat, and they have been known to capitulate to interplanetary councils to avoid the strain of conflict. Arcturuns are peaceful but they do not always agree, and there are times when families or communities need to have extended meetings in order to sort out their differences of opinion. However, differences in opinion are always exchanged in a respectful manner, and there will never be the need for war or violence as a result. There are no weapons on Arcturus as the thought of harming a fellow being would be abhorrent to them and would never enter into their realm of consciousness. As with Orionions and Siriuns, Arcturuns do not have egos as humans do, however, their temperaments are not as formal, calculating or 'cold' as their alien counterparts. They 'feel' in a way that Orionions and Siriuns do not, but it is also not in the emotional way that humans do. Their warmth comes from their heartspace and their connection to Source rather than from any emotional or mental state.

The message for Earth from Arcturus is simple and straightforward: do not allow yourself to become entangled in the affairs of others or to worry about events that you have no control over. Live each moment as it comes and accept yourself and others for who you are. When you are in your own truth and accepting of it, there is nothing that anyone else can do or say to harm you. Acceptance is the biggest gateway to peace, because acceptance allows one to feel at peace with oneself, with others and with any situation. Through acceptance comes love, and love will lead one into the state of oneness. This state allows everyone to feel connected, safe and loved, thus there will never be any need to harm another or feel unsafe. We are all one, even though we have different personalities, features, likes and dislikes. In the energy of the Creator we are all perfect, totally loved and cherished. This is the philosophy underlying the Arcturun way of life, and it is what they wish every human on Earth to know and experience.

That is all.

CHAPTER 15
Tourous

Tourous is a planet at the far, northern point of a galaxy two galaxies away from Earth. The planet is ninety percent water and the land is mountainous, craggy and very rough. The people are cave dwellers who have adapted to the harsh conditions by developing long, shaggy fur and long arms and legs, much the same as apes on Earth. They are much larger in stature than people on Earth and much more peaceful. In many ways they are more primitive than man in their ways and in their living conditions, perhaps akin to cavemen at the dawn of time on Earth.

The climate on Tourous is fairly calm and the temperature quite warm most of the time. The atmosphere is extremely thick and dense which keeps the warmth from their sun on the surface much longer than on Earth. There is little rain on Tourous, so when it does rain the people make sure to catch it efficiently. The water on the planet is brackish and undrinkable, but the people have developed efficient water filter systems. There are few plants on the land, and no food sources either, so the people eat primarily from the surrounding seas which contain a variety or plankton, small fish and plant life. The population of Tourous is relatively small in comparison to Earth, even though the planet has a surface area that is roughly the size of Mars. There are some people on Tourous who have adapted to life on the water, although they are considered outcasts by the land-dwellers and lead relatively separate lives. All people on Tourous live sustainably because they have large breeding areas for sea plant and animal life. They recycle water and waste, and their sewerage systems are simple but effective.

People on Tourous mostly live under the ground in large community caves. The sea dwellers live in rudimentary dwellings on top of the water and do not use the land much. There is a central living and eating area with family units off the central space. People live in families that consist of males and females, children and extended families. Sex is conducted much the same as on Earth with some differences, as the anatomy of the people are not exactly the same as humans. There are approximately 200 family communities on the planet. Inter-marriage between families is not permitted, and there are several times in the planet's rotation when large community gatherings occur for matches to be made for mating. Privacy is not an issue on Tourous and the people mate more like animals than humans on Earth — it is just accepted as a natural act and there is no shame or embarrassment in viewing other couples having sex close by!

Tourous is not a part of the IPGF as their communication and travel technologies are too primitive; they are therefore isolated without communication with other beings in the universe, just as Earth is. They are a relatively peaceful people but they do occasionally have disputes between communities which are generally over food sources and water supplies. However, they settle disputes through discussions and community forums, and once decisions are made there is no more argument. There is no government or High Council system on Tourous, but communities all have a say in matters and send delegates to meet with other communities when the needs arise. Food is grown and shared as a matter of course and no money ever changes hands. All is provided by the sea and the people share it without discussion.

The point of this chapter is to highlight the fact that not all 'aliens' in the universe are advanced races and capable of space travel and super technologies. The planet Tourous is, in many ways, like Earth at the beginning of its journey, but it already seems to have learnt the lessons of survival and communion with its planet without the need to plunge into war and conflict. The absence of the need for money is a major factor in the ability of the people to remain peaceful, yet it is more than that —they are happy with their lot. They accept their circumstances and each other, and they live their lives in order to survive — Tourous would be one of the harshest planets in the universe in terms of sustaining life.

Life is tough but simple on Tourous. Nothing changes, but that may be their biggest secret. Survival is the biggest issue on the planet, and the people know they need to work together in order to maintain sustainable and comfortable living conditions. Cooperation is the key to the people's survival on this planet and they do it without major government or restrictions. They abide by spiritual law and maintain the utmost respect for their planet for all it provides for them. In many ways humans may view Tourousians as primitive and animalistic, but if you were to consider the animal world on Earth you would see that all is always in order and there is no room for ego or discussion in the hierarchy of each species. Animals live their lives according to instinct and reactions to their environment, and so it is with the people of Tourous. In living this way they also ensure their own survival because they will never know the need to resort to war or violence — it is simply not written into their chemistry.

Humans could learn valuable lessons from the people of Tourous. They are kind and generous while being brave and fearless. They are connected to and respect the land and sea and all that is given to them; they do mourn what they lack as they have no need for anything above which is already provided. They accept themselves and each other and never question the culture that has been established. They consider themselves all one and the same, and there is no question over the sharing of resources, as long as it is equitable and fair. If it is not it is sorted out quickly and according to the hierarchy of order that is well established in their culture. The differences between the land and sea dwellers is not a problem and causes no divisions, and if there is ever a need to communicate with each other it is done so with the utmost respect.

Life on any planet in the universe works within a structure of order that has been naturally created and is intricate in its patterns of interaction. Natural hierarchies and semiotic relationships all work to create harmony and balance between living species. When all is kept the way it was created there can be no disequilibrium, and life on the planet will always run smoothly. This will be the case even with the presence of a species with higher intelligence as long as that species does not consider itself more worthy of respect than any other. That is how humans have created such an imbalance on Earth, not just by disrespecting lower forms of life on the planet, but also each other. By considering one race dominant over all others humans have caused a rift in their entire species that has consequently resulted in major imbalances in the vibrational patterns of the natural world. Without order there is chaos, and chaos in one species cannot ever be contained, as it will ripple out and impact the entire world.

Tourous is on its path of evolution just as Earth has been and its beginnings may seem similar to that of the apes and cavemen. There is one major differing factor which is most likely to keep Tourous from ever plunging into a state of war and separation like Earth has and that factor is that the natural order of the planet has been maintained through the people respecting the planet and each other. When imbalances occur, all is done to right them again so that the natural vibrational patterns of all co-existing on the planet, whether it be of animal, plant or mineral origin, can continue to harmonise with, not work against, each other. That is all it takes to keep an entire planet in harmony and a state of oneness, no matter how intelligent or primitive it is. The Earth would do well to learn this. It is so.

CHAPTER 16
The Pleiades Star Command

The Pleiadien star system contains life, but not as humans would know it. The people who live within the Pleiades are Star People and are a very intelligent consciousness without holding physical form. Their intellect is well known and held of the highest regard by the IPGF, and their contribution to the alliance of planets and star systems has been invaluable.

Pleiadiens are not like Shadow People — they do not form their own planet and they do not travel the universe in search of wisdom. Pleiadiens already hold all the wisdom they need, and they use this wisely and for the greater good of their star system and their 'people'. Their existence may not be physical, but it is of essence and creates form through intent; that is, the energy created through their vibrational thought patterns and conscious intentions creates matter and energy that can be seen and touched.

There are seven stars in the Pleiades star system, two of which hold the consciousness of the Star People. The alliance with the IPGF has been long standing, and there are many stories which could be told about the state of their relationship before peaceful resolutions were attained many eons ago. The greatest story to tell, however, is the one that is unfolding now, and that is the one we will focus on, for the Star People have no 'way of life' to report on as such, rather than a 'way of being' that is reflected in the purposeful way they interact with the IPGF, the high councils of planets within the federation, and the purposeful agenda under which all of their dealings are underpinned.

All existing Pleiadien consciousness forms part of the Pleiadien Star Command. They are all part and parcel of the military-style existence of intelligence on the two stars where they reside. Their whole focus is on maintaining order within their part of the galaxy, for peace was a long time in the making and has become a way of life that they wish to maintain. Their alliance with the IPGF has been a worthwhile one, for they have gained supreme intelligence and understanding of different ways of life within the universe and their ability to transcend cultural and language barriers has been second to none. Their understanding of the human consciousness is also superior, and the disorderly nature of much of the human existence is a parody of the orderly nature of the rest of the universe. Although the intelligence of the Pleiadian mind-stream is not affected by ego in any way, the ability to harness the essence of unconditional love that underpins all of creation has allowed the Pleiadien consciousness to be empathetic to the human plight, connecting to all of the emotions and feelings that exist in the universal collective consciousness and reducing it all down to a numerical equation! The Pleiadien intellect has developed equations for both the saviour and destruction of mankind — recipes, if you will, either for complete disaster or for ascension, and they are now, more than ever, willing to translate these to those Wayshowers and Lightworkers who are ready to listen.

It may seem absurd that emotions and feelings can be written as a mathematical equation, but it is wise to remember that with order everything remains symbiotic, semiotic and in divine flow. Emotions create turmoil and disequilibrium because they distort factual reality into emotional fantasy, causing the human to lose sight of the facts underlying the situation, the consequences for taking certain actions and the impact that their words and deeds may have on the world and those close to them. When feelings and emotions, which cannot be measured and which can be chaotic in nature, are translated into numeric sequences, they become orderly, measurable and controllable. Suddenly, to be human, with the whole spectrum of feelings and emotions that the human ego can possibly feel and show, can also be equated to the alien psyche, which understands love and oneness without the complications of emotions, and that is a powerful thing.

In conjunction with Earth's sister planets Sirius, Orion and Arcturus, and with the assistance of the IPGF, the Pleiadien consciousness now streams forth with guidance and assistance on how humans may rise above the lower vibrations of their egos. They wish to do this while still maintaining the essential nature of the human ego, which allows it to give and receive love freely with compassion, empathy and goodwill to his fellow man. There are people on Earth who have been accessing the mind streaming of the Pleiadien consciousness, but for the most part their existence has been largely unknown. Now is the time for their knowledge to be given and received.

It has been explained to you that the universe has been created on the foundation of unconditional love. Picture, if you will, the love of the Creator encapsulated in each atom, in every particle, rock, asteroid, planet, star and galaxy in the entire universe. How would it look, this unconditional love? What does love even look like? How does it feel? What IS love exactly? Without any measurable data, as it were, it is difficult to capture this love or to even visualise it, considering that rocks, asteroids and stars are made of solid matter that seems as far removed from love as anything could be. The Pleiadien consciousness now wishes you to remember the deepest and most joyful love experience you have ever had, the one that had your heart bursting out of your chest. It may be the time you were deepest in love, but it may also be a time when you loved a puppy or that you felt totally loved and cared for. The emotion is so wonderful and so profound that it encompasses your entire being. In the time of creation of this love, there are no words, and maybe even no emotions, to describe it. It just is.

The love of the universe is so. It simply is, and it is encapsulated within ever atom of everything that exists or that ever existed. In this way, all humans are love as well, because the seed of creation is within all of you and is underpinned with the unconditional love of the Creator. There is no emotion in this love because it just is. In this way it is possible to take the chaos out of the human emotion around feeling love, and therefore it is possible to do this around every other emotion humans feel that lead to war and violence towards each other on Earth.

How can the Pleiadiens, or any beings on other planets, begin to help humans on Earth when the human emotions cause so much chaos and prevent humans from connecting to the unconditional love that is within each and every one of them? The answer is simple — believe it to be so, ask to receive guidance, and meditate! The answers will come to you in a way that you can understand, and this may be different for each person.

Feel love and be love. When your emotions are chaotic and threaten cloud your judgement, remember the Pleiadian Star Command and ask them to help you to overcome them. They will enter your consciousness with rational thought and calming influences, helping you to see the situation away from emotional turmoil. If all people could access this assistance, the Earth's ascension would be assured!

And so it is.

PART 3
The Keys to Ascension

CHAPTER 17
Rising Above the Ego

It is no secret that the world continues to battle, on a large scale, with duality. Good versus evil, right and wrong, bad and good, joyful and miserable are all terms used every day to describe events that are occurring around the globe. It is true, on a Third Dimensional level, that the tragedies occurring are truly horrendous and, in many cases, unjust. There is no comprehending the crimes and the accidents that take so many lives and that plunge the families left behind into grief and despair. Creator and all of the Masters send their love and compassion to those who are coping, or have had to cope, with loss and devastation in the past or at the present time.

The truth in the Third Dimension, however, is very different to that in the Fifth Dimension and at the level of oneness, for in this state there is no duality. Oneness is achieved when your consciousness combines with the universal collective consciousness in acceptance that all is one and that there is no separation. When you accept this as a fact, not just as a possibility or as a fallacy, then you will begin to know the truth of the Creator. There is no separating someone in Sudan and what is happening for them from another person in Australia or Canada or India. There is no separation from Creator to God to Buddha to Krishna or to Jehovah — they are all one and the same. All on Earth, be it plant, animal or human, is connected, whether it be consciously or subconsciously, to the Creator and to Mother Earth. This connection binds all who reside on the planet Earth to each other and, as a consequence, lays equal responsibility for all that occurs on Earth on each and every soul living on Earth at this time. To ponder this concept may be quite staggering for many, but for those whose spirituality has reached a level where such thoughts are familiar, it is a fact that they carry knowingly and, in many cases, solitarily.

The world is erupting with war, violence and hatred. Many people are being killed by extremist rebels who have taken 'justice' into their own hands and who will not accept any other point of view. In other parts of the world, people are dying of starvation due to extremes in weather conditions that are causing imbalances in water and food supplies. Many people are suddenly experiencing heightened anxiety, panic attacks, depression and thoughts of suicide. Earth is, in many cases, out of balance and could be described as a 'world of extremes'.

The many changes occurring on Earth in 2015 are in conjunction with, as a result of and are also in contrast to the many acts of terrorism and/or war occurring on Earth at this time. (It is also important to add here that any act against another's free will, including the 'lawful' killing of another under death penalty laws can also be considered terrorism because they are acts against humanity and are not in the energy of unconditional love and oneness.) The vibrations on Earth are seemingly at a low point due to many factions of humans who believe so strongly in their own convictions that they wish to dominate others and change the world to their way of thinking. They are under the illusion that their way is God's way, but this could not be further from the truth. Everyone has a right to believe whatever they wish, but when it inflicts upon the free will of others and compromises their safety, or even causes their death, they are transgressing spiritual law and invoking the cycle of karma which will change their destiny and bring about many consequences for lifetimes to come. So called 'terrorism' on Earth is not in the vibration of oneness and love which is the only energy that can be attributed to God, the Supreme Source of all creation. It is designed to create the lowest vibrations possible on Earth and to keep humans separated from their God-self.

Terrorism is the product of ego, not evil. It is the product of the mind, not the heart. It is also the product of the person who has never known unconditional love and who wishes to dominate and control others because that is the only way they have ever known 'love' to be. If things do not go their own way, they condemn, punish and force others to their own will, and then they cover their actions with the false claims that it is God's will. All of the negativity generated between humans comes from the ego which desires to tell you all that you are better than another or that you deserve more in life that what you have been given. When you are able to ignore the voice of the ego and understand that all in the universe is one, and therefore connected, you will also find it much easier to tolerate difference, to accept people for who they are and to love yourself and others unconditionally.

The vibration of terrorism and war is one of hatred. It is the lowest vibration known to mankind and is not recognised in the universe by other planets or alien beings. The fear that stems from these acts is holding the majority of the human race in the Third Dimension. Love is the only answer here. The more terrorism that raises its ugly head the more love will begin to pour out of the human collective consciousness. This will enrage those who wish only to control through fear, so that is why, for a time, it may seem that there is a growth in terrorism on Earth rather than a subsiding of it. Be patient, because the vibration of hatred can never match the vibration of love. The ascension of the Earth will continue to occur without those who choose to harm others to fuel their own egos, as people who have already been raising their vibrations out of the Third Dimension will refuse to be drawn into the web of deceit and lies. For those who can rise above this low vibration we ask that you harness and spread the light of the Creator to the world and beyond every day and at every opportunity. You may do this in countless ways, from as small an action as a warm smile to a stranger or the giving of a gift to a friend, to larger acts of campaigning against animal cruelty or running a homeless shelter. Sending love and light to the planet, to innocent people caught up in terrorism, to people who are sick and even to perpetrators themselves will make a very big difference to the vibrations held around the world. There are many hundreds of ways you can give and receive unconditional love to yourself and others, and it is imperative that the amount of love sent out from the heartspaces of humans exceeds the energy radiating from acts of hatred, terrorism and war that have been keeping the Earth in fear and in the control of darker forces.

Do not be deluded by all of the drama, grandstanding and bloodshed going on around the world because it is all like a magician's smoke screen. As those wishing to keep the world in darkness towards their own ends continue to rule with fear and mind control, people are awakening to the light and are coming into their power. There has been a mass awakening over the last three years and the grips of darkness are loosening. Those who refuse to be swayed by propaganda are waging their own war of sorts against the darkness that is spread by lies, domination and fear. They are sending love and light to the world, and the counteractive effect cannot be underestimated! Visualisation with intent is all that is needed to manifest change, and when it is sent with intent from a group the effect is magnified.

Love is all there is! All else is illusion and will only become reality if you believe it to be so. Do not buy into the illusion of darkness, because the duality of light and dark is not in the energy of the Creator. When you see, feel and become love you are one with God's light. Nothing else is real. Believe in love, even if you cannot believe in God. See love as the only energy that is real, and send it with purpose to the world. You cannot imagine how powerful that one act can be.

Your soul has lived many lives in many bodies, countries and eras. You may even have existed in a form other than human. Your spirit is of essence — it is of the Earth and it is of the Creator, whose light is of essence and is one and the same as yours. His love encompasses your spirit and burns within you as the Sacred Flame. As the essence of the light of the Creator you know only unconditional love. In the human form, you have experienced the many facets of ego that cause emotional pain and trauma, yet the essence of the Creator that is inexplicably linked to your own still burns within you. You are ever one with Him whether you know it or not. All is one, and one is the all.

We remind you now that whatever you are experiencing on Earth or have experienced in the past is part of your soul journey. The lessons you are learning and have learnt all form an important part of your soul growth towards enlightenment. Any burdens you bear as a consequence of these lessons and experiences will all melt away if you would only become one with Creator's light. In the energy of the Creator you will have the opportunity to view all that has gone before you from a higher perspective. Even if you have witnessed acts of intolerable cruelty, injustice and sadness, from the eyes of the Creator you can see that much has been chosen and only some acts are karmic, for there is no judgement from God the Creator on those who inflict pain and suffering on other souls. He loves all unconditionally and He guides all who have lost their way into darkness back into the light, no matter how many lifetimes it may take. The cruellest acts on Earth bring with them the greatest lessons. As much as these events encourage separation and disconnection from Source, there have been many instances where the reverse has been true. Man cannot maintain a lifetime of separation from God because God, the Creator, has never left! Oneness has been achieved already — it only needs each individual to recognise this fact and to begin living in such a way as to be ever in the light.

That is all it will take for the world to ascend into the Fifth Dimension.

The soul who chooses to live in darkness will be hungry for power. They will have succumbed to the illusions of the ego which tells them that their needs are greater and their lives are more worthy than others. They will believe that the world revolves around them and, because they cannot see that all souls are equal in the eyes of God, their empathy for others will be greatly diminished or non-existent. Manipulation of others for power and money is driven by an ego which is both dominant and dominated by service to self. There is nothing more important to a darker soul than its own needs and wants. Anything else is immaterial. The darkness is all - consuming and can be ravenous in its quest to engulf a weaker soul in its power. Those who succumb to the power that the darkness offers will find themselves on an ego trip of mammoth proportions, but there are consequences for choices made in service to self that intervenes on the free-will of others. There is no action that one can take based on selfish needs that will not have a karmic reaction or consequence, and the repercussions of karmic interventions on another person's free will be swift and monumental — at full force. All paths lead to the light, but some roads will be long and arduous if the choices made in this life, or indeed in earlier ones, have been made with the intention of harm and in the vibration of hatred and self-absorption.

The nature of the ego can be very dark. There are many urges that can pull a person into behaviours or habits that are not for their highest and best and which impact on others in a negative or anti-social way. When a person gives in to the urges and temptations that the ego offers they can be swayed off their spiritual path into another that is unknown and that leads straight to karmic repercussions. The ego is often described as 'the devil', and often for good reason. The ego, however, is not evil, and there is a reason all humans have one. The ego is the voice that tells you how great you are, and every human on Earth must hold self-belief to be able to hold their position in the world with confidence. A healthy ego is essential to allow you to love, accept and respect yourself as a valuable and valued member of society. An inflated ego, however, will allow your mind to play tricks on you and to tell you that you are better than others, more worthy and therefore exempt from the rules that would otherwise apply to all, including you.

In the energy of the Creator the ego accepts that all is one and that everyone is equal and the same. Therefore, every person will be treated with respect and generosity, accepted for their differences and loved unconditionally. In this energy the person will love themselves unconditionally and put themselves first when necessary but not at the expense of any other person. This is the big difference between the energy of the Creator and that on the Third Plane of Existence which is Earth. To be in this energy one must simply bring in the light of God, the Creator, into your crown, your heartspace or even into your mind — connecting is that simple.

Not all souls living on planets other than Earth have experienced the dark side of the ego or travelled down the path of self-service. Many others have, however, and some of those beings have chosen to return to their lives away from Earth because of the temptations and the hardships that such a road can bring. The positive side of having lived lives on Earth are the lessons one can learn that result in tremendous soul-growth. Many souls on Earth's sister planets and surrounds are much higher entities since living out their karma on Earth, and the knowledge they now offer to share can be of great assistance to those on Earth who have lost their way. Yes, the path of darkness is a choice, but sometimes it can become a self-serving prophesy that is difficult to move away from.

Between each lifetime, soul groups meet together to determine the next stage of their soul journeys. Should they reincarnate, and, if so, what lessons do they choose to learn next and what karma needs to be repaid? Will they choose to resolve their karma and move on, or do they have more to learn, even if it means a longer road to the light? There are many choices a soul must make, and these choices are always made in conjunction with the other souls who make up the particular soul-family that one belongs to. There is never any judgement, either from the Creator, the Masters of Light or one's soul family, for the choices one makes are for the purpose of learning and soul growth. If one has lost one's way, help is always there for the taking, should one choose to accept it. If not, it will still be there until such time that it is accepted. No soul family ever questions the choices of their kin, even if in human form they appear to. Anyone that humans meet throughout their lifetime will have a purpose for being there, whether it be to assist the person to learn or to resolve a lesson, to spark a new lesson or to repay or resolve karma. There is no chance in any meeting, and there is no human relationship, positive or negative, that can be called a coincidence. If you feel a particular connection with a stranger or acquaintance and then go on to develop a strong friendship or relationship with them, chances are they are part of your soul family.

It may seem likely to humans that all souls in ethereal form are 'good' and of a trustworthy nature, but anyone who has encountered an 'evil spirit' is unlikely to agree with you! 'Good' and 'evil' are terms of duality and useful in human vocabulary to describe the state of people or things in positive or negative ways. No spirit is essentially evil, as it originally came from the light, and it will eventually go back to the light. But a soul who has lost its way and its connection to Source will be easily consumed by the lure of the power of the dark, and it may take many lives and deaths on the Earthly plane to regain its connection again. In between lives it is the vibration of the soul that determines the dimension and the plane in which it resides. There are many lower depths of the Fourth Plane, or the Spirit World, in which lower vibratory souls must reside until they have made conscious efforts to regain their connection to Creator and to resolve their Earthly karma. The lower Fourth Plane is not a place for the faint hearted, and it is unwise for any human to access the Fourth Plane at all without first connecting to the Creator's light.

No-one has the right to stop any soul from making choices based on their free will, unless those choices break spiritual law and impinge on the rights of others. The judgement one receives on Earth for one's actions is not mirrored in the ethereal kingdom, but there is a process for reviewing one's life and the choices one has made throughout. The smallest kindness will seem mountainous in one's life review, as will the slightest travesty. If there has been a major incident that has impacted on or taken another's life, the grief that one's soul will feel will be enough of a sentence without any punishment or retribution from God. Thus begins the road the soul chooses, either the long or the short way to the light. The choices that are made after and before life will greatly impact the path one takes during a lifetime, but a lifetime that is written is always subject to other influential factors that the soul is too weak to resist.

As a soldier works its way through the ranks, so a spirit grows and evolves. Some do it very quickly, but for others it is a slow and often arduous journey. It matters not to the Creator, who sees all in the universe with unconditional love and oneness. Whichever path you choose, know that you are one with Creator and the all and that will never change. He loves you unconditionally, and his love just is.

It is so.

CHAPTER 18
Oneness

Oneness is unity. It is where all things in the universe are connected by infinite threads with no separation between them. Oneness is awareness of self in the eyes of the Creator, who sees all his children as one with Him and holds them in perfection. When you are one with the Creator you are loved unconditionally in all areas of your life. There is no judgement or condemnation, only love and light. To achieve oneness you need do nothing, for it is already so! However, to live your life in full consciousness of oneness is another matter. Bring the light of the Creator into your heartspace, into your breath and into your being. Hold His light as love and feel it as your love also, for the love of the Creator is also your own. Know that the love of the Creator lives and breathes in all things and there is nothing that is separate from Him or that is not loved by Him. When you know the unconditional love of the Creator and live within His light you will also see everything from a place of love. One cannot judge others when one lives in the light and love of the Creator, nor can one judge oneself, because the Creator knows no such state.

Oneness is not a state of mind nor even a consciousness — it is a truth of the universe. Everything in the universe is connected — there is nothing or no-one that is not united. Separateness is a myth that has been fostered on Earth to keep those in power in control of the masses, but on most other planets oneness is embraced as a natural way of life.

People on Earth who have lived lives on either Orion, Arcturus or Sirius have experienced what it is to live in harmony. Their souls know how to protect their planet and how to live without inflicting harm on another living being. They have lived without ego, but that is not to say that all humans who are descendants of Orion, Sirius and Arcturus are now peaceful beings. Many are, of course, but the human ego is a powerful force that is capable of overcoming the purest of souls. That is why Siriuns, Orionions and Arcturuns reincarnate on Earth, so as to experience the force of the ego and to learn the lessons that come from living in a harsh and judgemental environment. Not all beings who come to Earth to experience life here return and some, in contrast, never return to their home planets. Many, however, traverse the universe experiencing life on all planets, and their souls are richer and wiser for the experience. It is these souls who are the wayshowers of the world at this time. They are awakening to their gifts and to the realities of ascension before them. They are also hearing the call from the ethereal planes to assist in the awakening and ascension of Mother Earth and its people. The time has come to draw on their universal knowledge and to connect to the oneness of the universe to bring Earth back to its ascended state and into oneness with the universe as a whole. Their brothers and sisters on Orion and Sirius are instrumental in bringing forth the information that is needed now that the alignment of Earth to these planets has occurred.

It is not necessary to consciously hear or see every piece of information that is being downloaded to people on Earth who are ready to receive it. All you need to know is that there is much encoded information coming to Earth that is helping people to raise their vibrations to the ascended state necessary to bring Earth out of conflict, hatred and greed. Mother Earth is also relinquishing her secrets and is doing everything she can to assist the wayshowers to transmit and interpret universal knowledge and wisdom to others. There are powerful vortexes of energy being sent and received at different times of the year in alignment with the moon that will bring about the huge energy shifts that are needed to bring the Earth to a state of oneness.

Siriuns, Arcturuns and Orionions do not know the darkness because they are centred in their heart spaces at all times. Their focus, as for Pleiadians, is on the greater good for all, which automatically brings them into the light. Because they are not concerned with self, their thoughts, actions and intentions are always of the highest vibration. Even though they may not be consciously connected with Source, they are always connected to the Creator because they are forever connected to themselves. Their intentions are formed out of unconditional love for themselves and their community. In that way they live in the light, and they wish to communicate this to you on Earth now in order to assist humans to raise their energies to a higher consciousness.

Dark days on Earth are as a result of negative energies and interactions between humans. The illusion of separation allows people to believe they are acting alone and that their thoughts and actions have no consequences on anyone around them. This is, of course, a fallacy because there is no separation, only oneness. To live in the light is to know that all on Earth and in the universe is one, and that to think, say or do anything with any intention lower than love is to immediately put one and those around you in a state of imbalance. Earth has been out of balance for centuries now, but the time is nigh when the pendulum will cease to swing and will stop, dead centre, bringing all those who have brought in their Lightbodies to a state of oneness and peace. This is how Siriuns and, indeed, all other planets in the alliance live, making the current ways on Earth foreign and distressing.

There has been much talk of late about New Age, Ascension and Lightbodies, and many people on Earth, particularly those whose faith lies embedded in religion, cannot align their thoughts or beliefs to such concepts. It is not necessary to be consciously thinking and believing in the New Age to be in a state of ascension because it is your vibration that will determine whether you are in a third, fourth or fifth dimensional state. It is the intent of your thoughts and actions that determine your vibrations. Everything, after all, is a state of consciousness and the higher your consciousness, the higher your vibration. When your vibration matches that of Fifth Dimensional energy you have reached the ascended state and have brought in your Lightbody.

Siriuns and Orionions are in their Lightbodies as a matter of course. They are also in their physical bodies, but only as a vehicle to maintaining life on Sirius for the good of the planet and all who dwell upon it. The physical body is merely a tool for learning, and people of the sister planets do learn lessons, if not personal ones. They learn lessons for the greater good, and their unified knowledge is what keeps the vibration of the colony so high. Sirius is one of the great teaching planets — many humans have lived lives on Sirius, and the knowledge those people bring with them will be of great service to Earth if they are willing to access it through their higher self. When former Siriuns or Orionions, who are now living as humans, bring their knowledge to Earth in the highest and best way, the vibrational change to the Earth's human consciousness will be immense.

As part of their agreement with universal inter-galactic federations, the Siriun Council wishes to impart knowledge in order to assist humans to reach the state of ascension; — a state in which Siriuns and Orionions exist in as a matter of course. They do so willingly and from their heart spaces to yours. Allow your heart to receive these messages with love.

Oneness is achieved through the state of your consciousness. Pleiadians, Siriuns and Orionions achieve this with ease. Oneness is part of their upbringing but also a state they are born in. People on these planets never feel the pull of separation as so many of you on Earth do. Beings from other planets such as Arcturus find they need to work a little harder to achieve a state of oneness, only because they have had histories of war and of unrest. They have, however, achieved this state through communion with each other and the International Galactic Federation of Peace, who have counselled them and helped them to resolve the past.

Oneness is not taught as separatism is in your world. Oneness just is. It is the universal state, and any other state outside of it works against the flow of the universe. This is why there is so much imbalance on Earth. The figure who was sent to save you, The Christ, is the ultimate example of the state of oneness. He lived it, he spoke it and he taught it. He lives still, in the hearts, bodies and minds of all of you. His consciousness, the Christ Consciousness, oversees the oneness of the universe because the energy of this consciousness is love — unconditional, pure and infinite. Thus, the symbol of this consciousness is the infinity symbol.

Love just is, as oneness just is. You cannot put any other label on them. They are not conditions, they just are, because the universe has been created on the basis that all is one and oneness cannot be achieved without the presence of unconditional love. This is the key to oneness, and the only way to save the world at this time.

It has taken many years of lessons and disconnection for man to come back to the realisation that the only way forward is to come together in peace and harmony. It is almost too late, but it can be done. We are here to assist in any way we can. Please allow us this honour.

Living in a state of oneness can literally save the planet Earth. Here are some of the main tools you can personally use to take your energies to the Fifth Dimension:

> See the world as a unified force that is connected to you. Oneness unifies whereas belief in separateness judges and crucifies.

> Love yourself. When you love and value yourself you will treat yourself with the utmost respect. You will then, in turn, respect all of those around you, including plants, animals and the Earth.

> Think with your heart rather than with your mind. Your mind is your greatest weapon and also your greatest enemy. It has the potential to lead you into ego which can make you believe lies and falsehoods. What you believe will affect how you perceive the world. Stepping out of ego is the most powerful tool in

the path to ascension. See everything from a higher perspective, not how it affects you personally.

- Raise your vibrations. See everything through a positive lense and with love. The higher your vibrations, the more positive your energies will be. When you change your mindset, the world around you will respond.

- Do not enter into drama. It is only the product of ego and will work to keep your vibrations and energies low.

- Remember that everything happens for a reason and that you are here to learn. Choose your lessons wisely and learn from them. This is the way all souls grow and evolve.

- Treasure Mother Earth. See everything as sacred. Treat everything on Earth as you would wish to be treated.

- Eat healthy food. A healthy mind stems from a healthy body. Bless and give thanks for your food and for the animals who gave up their lives for your nutrition. Ask a plant's permission before you pick its fruit and the vibration of nutrition returned to you will be much higher.

- Keep away from pesticides and chemicals. Eat and use food and products that are as close to nature as possible.

- Choose your thoughts and words carefully. Everything you do, say and think creates your reality and directly affects the Universal Consciousness.

- Keep grounded by being present in the moment. Release the energies of the past and leave the future to run its course.

- Release all judgement of yourself and of others. Every human on Earth treads their own path and has their own lessons to learn. You will resonate with some and feel alienated from others. Whether you believe or agree with another person is of no consequence. Accept all for who they are and love them unconditionally. You will receive the same treatment from them, and the vibrations of the world will be greatly increased.

- See each day of your life on Earth as a gift, not a right. Drink in the wonders of life as they occur all around you.

- Be grateful for all that you have, no matter how little. Practising gratitude as a daily ritual will bring abundance into your life much more quickly and with greater force.

- Give away that which you desire. It will come back to you threefold.

- Trust in the laws of the universe. The universe will always work for you, whether it be in a positive or negative way. What you put out will come back to you in mirrored form.

- Be clear on your intentions, but make sure they are positive, because karma still exists for those whose intentions invade the free will of others.

- Be in a state of oneness, for the truth will be unveiled to you when you are in your own truth and in a state of peace and love. Nothing is separate - it is all given and all in the universe are joined in consciousness.

As the energies of Ascension continued to quicken, people may be experiencing heightened emotions and reactions. One of the causes could be attributed to regular disruptions to or increases in magnetic energy from the sun that can upset some people's equilibrium. Another reason could be sensitivity to Mother Earth as she goes through extremes of weather, energy in her collective consciousness and in human vibrations and, because all in the universe is connected and one, those who are tuned in or who are particularly sensitive and empathic to the energies of others will find that they cannot avoid picking up these vibrations. A third reason is that the energies of ascension are strengthening and speeding up. Those who are not in integrity will find themselves exposed, and those people who are still learning lessons will suddenly find the lesson right in front of them, needing to be faced and learnt. Others who have not paid attention to keeping their chakras and auras clear may experience physical illness and symptoms in response to the disrupted energies.

If you are overly sensitive to the heightened vibrations in the world at this time there are several courses of action we recommend that you take. One is to remain vigilant in grounding and sealing your energy fields every day. Send your energy into Mother Earth in the morning and make sure that you remain grounded throughout the day. Ask Creator, your angels or the Masters of Light to protect your auric field with a shield of golden light, and protect this shield by cutting ties with people with whom you come into close contact with throughout the day. You may also like to carry a crystal that resonates with you for extra protection. The other important thing to do is to remove your emotional energy from the dramas of the world. Remember that all, including slaughter and violence, is an illusion and a way of learning lessons or repaying karmic debt. Attempt to see the bigger picture rather than the daily drama. Above all, send love and healing to yourself and to the world. Bring in the light of the Creator; sit in it, send it and emanate it from the depths of your being. The unconditional love of the Supreme Source is the only way the energies of war, hatred and separation can be reversed and changed to that of ascension, peace and oneness.

And so it is.

CHAPTER 19
Learning to Just Be

Humans are busy doing. You worry about the future and you agonise over the past. The present often just passes you by because you are not present in the present. Humans often do life rather than live it, and when you are ready to experience all that life has to offer it is sometimes too late — you may be too old or the chance has gone and left you behind.

Trees just are. They exist in the now and put their roots into the soil of Mother Earth with intent. They grow strong and sure, holding the energy in their own space with certainty and pride. Although their life depends upon the rain and the sun for survival, their energy is always the same, never fluctuating or doubting. Trees are a life-force on which humans would do well to model their own consciousness, as it would enable you to stand your ground, live in the moment and with strong intention, being sure of your purpose for living and holding the space for others to come to in need. When you just are, living live with purpose and intent for the now, you are in Divine Flow and will then attract all that the universe has to offer you. You will be able to do so without blocking it with worry and anxiety about things you have no control over.

A tree is a shelter and a haven for all who depend on it. Insect, animals, birds and people alike depend on trees for food and shelter, and the strength emitted in the tree's energy is very reassuring and calming. If the tree is happy and content, the energy it emits reflects its state of health and wellbeing and henceforth radiates it out to the world. If, however, the tree is starved for nutrients and water, is being attacked by parasites or stifled by weeds, the energy it emits will be very different and act to repel, rather than attract, creatures and humans.

The same is to be said about the energy that humans radiate out to the world. The state of your mind and your physical health will directly affect the vibrational frequency of your energy. The higher your vibrations, the more likely you are to attract abundance in all things: wealth, food, friends, love and so on. The lower the frequency of your energy the likelihood that you will attract abundance decreases, mainly because your feelings of health and wellbeing will be low and your negativity towards life will be high. Worry, anxiety, immersion in drama, ill health and negative emotions such as hatred, resentment and anger will all serve to lower your vibrations, and your energy will repel people and the abundance the universe has to offer.

It may sound cliché, but one of the 'secrets' of the universe and way to ascension it to just be — be like a tree and all will come to you as it should! To be happy and content in yourself and with what you have already created in your life is to project love and contentment out into the world and the universe. What you give out will come back to you in equal measure, and may even be magnified if you have given of your heart with pure intention and no expectation. All in the universe is given freely with no expectation of return, so when you hold the same energy it will be returned to you in abundance.

The laws of the universe act upon polarity — as above, so below. As the pendulum swings one way it must return and swing the opposite way. 'Opposites attract' is not just a random saying, but a statement of universal law. If you put into action an event which impacts upon the health and wellbeing of others, the pendulum will bring that energy back to you with an unexpected force that will send your life into a tailspin. If, however, you give of your abundance and love freely and willingly, when the pendulum comes back to you it will bring with it love, abundance and joy in equal and unqualified measure. There is no stopping the force of nature nor the changing of the tide. So it is with spiritual law — for every action there is an equal and opposite reaction. For every decision you make there is a consequence, and for every consequence there is a chain reaction that has nothing to do with circumstance or coincidence — all that occurs does so because of spiritual law.

The laws of nature are that all is in perfect balance. All life forces upon the planet, including human beings, have been created to live symbiotically and in perfect harmony with each other. The cyclic nature of the seasons and of life itself mean that all works together in unison and is as it should. With no intervention, nature is a perfect example of creation — everything just is. However, as man inflicts his ego upon the world he disrupts the harmony and synchronicity of nature and of the systems within his own body. The urgency of time and money puts the natural world into chaos, and the battles being fought on the astral plane are as a direct result of man's wish to control and profit, rather than to exist in harmony with his kind and with the planet as a whole.

Meditation is the key to bringing yourself and body back into balance and connected to the natural rhythms of your body and the world. It is the key to beginning your ascent into the fifth Dimension, because the more you are connected to the Divine Source, to Mother Earth and are centred in your own being, the more aware you will become of yourself as a divine, spiritual being who has chosen to have a human experience. You will also become aware of the fact that you have never been alone, and that all you need to do is to ask for help — it will be given immediately. The world is your oyster, but not for exploitation. The beauty of nature is also within you — allow your own beauty from your soul to blossom outwards and begin the wonderful journey of self-discovery, self-realisation, self-awakening and connection to the all.

You will be amazed.

And so it is.

CHAPTER 20
New Beginnings

The messages in this book may be new to many, and we know that many of you may find our words unbelievable. However, there are many more people who will have been waiting a long time to read them, and it is to believers that we now speak. Whether our messages are believed or not, the universe is as we have described and the opportunity for ascension into the Fifth Dimension is now upon the Earth. There will not be another opportunity again, a fact which increases the urgency of spreading universal truths throughout the human population.

It is time now for humans to think beyond 'global' collaboration and to begin considering 'universal' collaboration. There is much wisdom held in the higher selves of humans walking the planet, but the denser energy is preventing true connection for many. By asking the Creator, the Masters of Light and your alien relatives to assist you to reach higher dimensions in your thoughts and actions you will become much more able to access the knowledge that you intrinsically hold but are unaware of in your conscious thoughts.

We, your alien neighbours and the Masters of Light, harnessing the power of the Supreme Creator, have come together in a united force to assist Earth to overcome fear and darkness and to move forwards into joyful oneness. We do not wish to change the essence of the human nature, for that is what makes you essentially unique to other life forms in the galaxy and beyond. We may have made it sound as if the nature of the ego is essentially evil, and we apologise if this is the case. To have an ego is to be able to feel emotion, and this in itself is a gift that most other races do not have. To feel and give love from the heart is a different reality to alien races. They know love yet they do not really feel it. It does not move them, hurt them or make them feel utter joy as it does a human. To have an ego and to know how important you are in relation to everything else around you is also a gift, as long as this sense of importance does not become over-inflated. To hold yourself as equal to all else is to see value in life and in your contribution to it and, indeed, your life on Earth as a wondrous gift. To consider others as important as oneself is to move beyond the ego and closer to oneness, for all humans are infinitely connected through the unconditional love of the Creator. To love yourself unconditionally is to love God, and vice versa — when you can love yourself this way you can also love others accordingly.

It may seem that there is a long way to go in terms of reaching the ascended state on Earth currently. This state is, of course, a state of world peace and oneness with the Creator that will see an end to all wars and bring the human consciousness into sync with itself and the all. Although it seems impossible, you must believe it can be so, because to deny ascension is to create the opposite reality. When all seems lost and hopeless it is difficult to see beyond the reality of the moment. However, if you were to meditate and to connect with the light of the Creator you would see beyond the realities of the physical world and know how it feels to be loved unconditionally. This love is like no other, and it is your right to feel it in every cell to the core of your being. When you know this love, and accept it as your divine right, you will radiate it out to others and the world. God is within every one of you and His love reaches the world through the heartspace of every human who has become conscious of their oneness with Him. In this way the world will ascend, and it is happening faster than you may think.

If you are able to see beyond the physical reality, you will also realise how much has changed in the world since ascension on the 12/12/12, particularly in the human psyche. There is much more awareness of the underhanded dealings of the dark forces, and united outrage at the atrocities that are still being inflicted on the innocent and the young. There is also a calling to arms, as it were, of environmentalists and Earth healers who are bringing much light and love into the united consciousness. The world is awakening, and with this awareness ascension is slowly occurring. While the acts of terrorism are designed to control the populations through fear and control, the very opposite is increasingly becoming a reality — people are saying 'no.' People are recognising that God would never inflict such pain and suffering upon others and are banding together as a united front against the bullying that encompasses all forms of terrorism and dictatorship. The outpouring of grief and rage at the many injustices inflicted upon the innocent has created a swell of love and unity between strangers and friends alike. The more humans uniting in the face of adversity the more the scales are tipping in favour of ascension. The rising of the Earth into the Fifth Dimension depends on each and every one of you. Know that the Masters of Light and the Inter-Planetary Galactic Federation are here to assist you to find the love of the Creator in yourselves, in others and in the world around you.

Connection to and collaboration with the Inter-Planetary Galactic Federation, the Pleiadian Star Command, planetary High Councils and the use of the Siriun

Blue Flame is best conducted by individuals rather than on-masse or by governments, because the general population are either distrusting of aliens or unaware of their existence. In addition, a repetition of past mistakes and injustices by government agencies and those working against ascension is highly likely and potentially disastrous. Lightworkers who are committed to raising the vibrations of Earth into the Fifth Dimension can meditate on their own or in trustworthy groups to connect to the Federation and to ask for help. Alternatively, they can also connect with councils from any planet within the Federation and assistance will be given. We especially encourage the use of the Siriun Blue Flame for this purpose.

Humans have been given the opportunity to save the Earth, and the choices each one of you makes in your present incarnation could not be more important at this time. Every thought, word and deed creates, and it is not too late to change what has already been created. All it will take is a united force against those who have chosen to work against humanity. Nothing can be done to sway their decisions, but they are a minority in comparison to the rest of the Earth's population. As more people awaken, so the tide will turn, the pendulum will swing and the human consciousness will rise towards enlightenment.

The survival of Mother Earth is depending upon it.

Love is all around you. It is within you. You ARE love. The very essence of you is love, and it starts with the Creator. When you can see everything as the Creator sees it then you will start to realise that nothing is more important than life itself, because, within the seed of life is creation, and the seed of creation is the Adamantine Particle. When you breathe in the Adamantine Particle, you are creating with love and intention. You are seeing love, breathing in and out love and being love. Call to Jesus to bring you to the light as that has always been His purpose: to live in the light, to be the light and to lead you to the light. His love is within every one of you, and when you can feel it in your heartspace the road to the light will be shorter.

The saviour of the world is love. There is no need for Jesus to walk the Earth for a second time, because humanity will save itself when it breathes in love and becomes its own light. When you breathe in light and become the light for others, God's love will shine from within and thus upon the world like a beacon. No darkness can survive such brightness, and no vibration of hatred can sustain its rule. Love is the answer. It just is, and that is all there is.

We ARE the Masters of the Cosmic Council and members of the Inter-Plantetary Galactic Federation.

Blessings and love go with you.

2015

About The Author

Victoria came to know herself in spirit when she participated in a beginner's spiritual development course in 2008. She has since become a Reiki Master, an Advanced Theta® Healing practitioner and an expert psychic channel. A trained teacher, Victoria lives and works on the NW coast of Tasmania with her husband Richard. They have three adult boys. Victoria divides her time between teaching on class and running her small healing practice. On top of providing readings and healings by appointment, she facilitates courses to help others to step into their own spiritual/psychic gifts, writes a monthly spiritual newsletter and publishes regular messages from the Masters of Light on her channellings blog. Victoria has published two books: "Raising the Energies of Mother Earth Towards and After Ascension 2012: The Highest Truth." (2013, Balboa Press) and "Beyond Ascension 2012: Universal Truths." (2013, Balboa Press).

www.victoriacochrane.com

http://victoriacochrane44.com

www.reachingoutspiritualnews.blogspot.com

Printed in Australia
AUOC02n1217110416
275107AU00001B/2/P